Joe G. Henderson's

Guide to the Working Alaskan Malamute
Volume One: Birth to Three Years

Joe G. Henderson

All The Best of Hunts!
God Bless!!

Joe Henderson

ISBN: 9798653039492

Edited by Abel Editing
Graphic Design by Carla Hendrix

Dedicated to

My Beloved Wife Janice

Table of Contents

Introduction

When I was eight years old, images of Neil Armstrong wearing a big white spacesuit and walking on the moon inspired my adventurous spirit. Being so young and open-minded at the time, I figured there weren't limits to what a person could do. If a man could bounce around on the shiny moon above, then I could do something as incredible and amazing.

Somehow, by watching Neil's accomplishment, I put it together that if you wanted something badly enough, you could do it. Of course, my parents and others warned me there were in fact limits. I chose to ignore their talk and the limits themselves.

Long ago, I read a quotation that went something like this: Ordinary people have accomplished extraordinary things because they didn't know they couldn't. This statement sums up how I have lived my life. As a young man, I simply closed my ears to the suggestions that I had limitations and that my dreams were too far-fetched or impossible. The result was that my horizon opened wide. I saw nothing but possibilities. The world was waiting for me.

For those who don't know me, let me describe myself. I live in Alaska and have a passion for dogsledding. However, I haven't ever run the Iditarod, or any race for that matter. I do own dogs and they and I do dogsled for months at a time under conditions that are often harsher than what is experienced on the Yukon Quest and Iditarod races.

It's not that my dogs can't compete per se. But, they are a special breed and most competitive dogsledders don't use this breed to race because they are too large and too slow. Plus Alaskan malamutes have an unusual temperament that makes training difficult unless you know how to relate to them.

Alaskan malamutes are one of the most ancient dog breeds on Earth. Historically they are freighters, pack and draft animals. They are not physically designed for racing because they are large-framed dogs with dense muscles and bones. Alaskan huskies that are used for racing are small-framed, lean, and they have super-light bones. These traits allow them to run faster than heavy-weighted Alaskan malamutes. An apt comparison is the Clydesdale horse. You would never see the Kentucky Derby run by Clydesdales. Not only would a Clydesdale lose the race, but the animal would be injured in an effort to keep up with the competition.

That said, there are Alaskan malamute lines that are small, narrow- shouldered, and light-boned that can somewhat keep up in long-distance races, but that line is entirely different from the Alaskan malamutes that I own. And like small Alaskan huskies, the smaller and lighter-frame malamutes aren't suitable to long-distance Arctic travel and freighting.

For those of you who do enjoy running the smaller type of malamute or for those of you who enjoy running huskies for purposes other than racing, much of the training and sledding techniques discussed here will be of interest, applicable, and beneficial to your practice with your own dogs.

The three leaders from right to left, Farmer, Champ and Junior are poised to head-out.

For over three decades, my dog team and I have traveled during the dead of winter in Alaska's Arctic. Many expeditions were in support of transporting scientists' gear like weather stations. During the last ten years, however, my expeditions were focused on discovering and documenting traits that are required for Alaskan malamutes to travel and thrive in the Arctic. I believe this is pertinent to preserving the Alaskan malamute dog breed. If we don't identify Arctic-compatible traits and center our breeding program to highlight these traits, then we will certainly lose the breed.

Even though we have an American Kennel Club (AKC) standard as a general guideline for Alaskan malamutes' physical traits, I believe the authors should have had been more explicit in describing Arctic travel and freighting attributes. Authors of the AKC standard did not have extensive experience with Arctic travel by dog team, so it's reasonable to suggest the standard is not completely accurate and do not cover the full spectrum of traits that are required for Arctic travel, i.e., breaking trail and freighting. For example, the standards state "the rear legs [of Alaskan malamutes] are broad and heavily muscled." However, the standards don't go into precise detail about what "broad" means for these dogs so that breeders can be clearly aware of what to look for. Nor does the standard state that Alaskan malamutes should have a broad or wide chest. The widths of a dog's hip and chest are two of the most important traits for Arctic travel. Unfortunately, these traits are quickly disappearing from the breed because breeders aren't aware of the importance of the traits. The standards also state that the feet are "large" and "snowshoe type;" yet, these essential traits are being replaced with small round paws that are not conducive whatsoever to Arctic travel. This is concerning because even when the standards state that the feet should be "snowshoe type," some breeders are either ignoring the standards or misinterpreting them. And most people would also agree that the "heavy boned" trait is also becoming dangerously rare. If the Alaskan malamute breed becomes incompatible to Arctic travel

Circled is Alaska's Arctic or, North Slope, that cover a larger land mass than many countries

then it's safe to say we have lost the breed.

My dogs and I have crisscrossed the Arctic numerous times while breaking trail in two to six feet of snow during multi-month expeditions. And my team's successful Arctic expedition of four months is a record for the longest solo unassisted without resupply in recorded history. Nearly all of my multi-month (two to four months) expeditions were without resupply. I want to point this out because it exhibits how amazingly powerful malamutes, in general, really are. Try to imagine a team of any breed of dog you might know hauling two to four months of dogfood across the Arctic?

Alaska's northern Brooks Range, the so-called inaccessible region.

I sometimes find it difficult to wrap my head around the incredible strength of malamutes. But there's more to their ability than meets the eye. The secret is not toughness, although Alaskan malamutes are extremely tough. Rather, it's their unique personalities that help them endure. My specific training technique focuses on getting the best from them based on understanding their personalities. I discuss my unique approach to these strong animals in this book.

During the multi-month expeditions, my dogs and I travel every day regardless of temperature (except during fierce blizzards) and we camp every night in different locations. We have broken trails in regions of Alaska's Arctic where never a dog team has traveled in recorded history. It's just me and my team living and breaking trail in one of the most brutal environments on Earth. Mother Nature dishes out the good and bad—sometimes within the same day.

The team and I have camped under the blinking stars during the coldest temperatures recorded in North America and we have endured the worst blizzards in Alaska's history.

Tails up and waving with enthusiasm and excellent health!
Note: all photographs in this book were taken by Joe G. Henderson unless specified otherwise.

Facing these extreme challenges with my dogs has forced me to rethink the traditional ways of dog mushing and sled dog training. I realized that I needed to approach the craft from a different direction. I needed to go inside the hearts and minds of the dogs and focus my energy on doing my best to understand their unique characteristics. You might find it interesting that my study of these dogs has led me to devote most of my training energy on nurturing the psychological rather than physical abilities of these dogs.

This approach has made it possible for my team and me to travel effectively in the Arctic. Additionally, I modified a new sled and dog-hitch system that is highly efficient, and I built a multi-sled system that can accommodate 3,500-pound loads. Finally, I discovered useful Arctic trail-breaking traits and use these traits in my breeding program to help me select my teams. Taken together, these components make my particular training technique distinct from the modern-day sled dog training methods.

I believe the changes I have made are important, but I attribute 100% of my success to my dogs— to their naturally strong physiques, mental stamina, efficient metabolisms, and their most cherished and valuable trait of all—their cheerful warrior demeanors, which I will elaborate on throughout this book.

This photo shows the dogs "swimming" through deep snow while pulling the two heavily loaded freight-sleds

There is one additional note worth mentioning that ties the team and me together as one unit. It is that I rarely ride on the sled. I either snowshoe or ski ahead or behind the team. I basically run a marathon everyday while traveling. But, not everyone wishes to freeze their butts in the Arctic and snowshoe for miles and miles. Some mushers are passionate for competitive dog-powered sports and enjoy the thrill and speed that huskies produce. Some mushers want nothing more except easy sledding on silent winter trails with their best friends pulling to their hearts content. And other mushers (like me) want to explore the far reaches of the Arctic's frozen landscape while relying on their dogs for survival and companionship.

Although there are different ways to dogsled and there are different views and strategies for training dogs for dogsledding, we can all agree on our love of dogs and how we want the best for them. For this reason, it is good to acknowledge that as humans we can get a little frustrated when our beloved dogs don't behave how we have envisioned. We've all experienced this. It requires a world of patience to remedy. This is why—if you truly want the best for your dogs—it's important to train yourself first.

 Let me explain. When we look inside a dog's mind we'll find similar emotional patterns seen in humans, like happiness, sadness, love, hate, trust, and mistrust. Unlike humans though, dogs have an incredible sense of smell, up to 100,000 times stronger than ours. And, most fascinating, dogs can actually smell and react to the rise and fall of hormone levels in people. Hormones like oxytocin, dopamine, and serotonin are our happy or feel-good hormones. This is something to keep in mind when you're working with your dogs because their demeanor reflects yours. So when you're happy, they will be happy as well. And just like people, happy dogs are hard and loyal workers. They will exhibit extraordinary strength and loyalty when they are happy.

This last sentence is the foundation of my dog training strategies. And it begins when puppies open their tiny eyes for the first time and view the big wide world around them. In my training, from this early point forward, the natural mental strengths of my dogs are nurtured and preserved as I prepare them for a future in mushing, which they naturally love with passion.

In this first book of my series of three books, I will address the care of Alaskan malamutes from birth to three years and how to train them for dogsledding. The second book will discuss training and managing my dogs and dog sled team. I will also discuss the physical traits of malamutes that are best suited for Arctic travel. And the third book will cover my Arctic travel and sledding methods as well as the gear, clothing, and supplies I rely on for my multi-month expeditions. Additionally, in the second and third books, I will talk somewhat about what I do to prepare myself mentally and physically to be the best team player for my dogs.

There is so much I want to share with you.

So, let's get going!

Breaking trail in Alaska's Arctic

Chapter 1: My Inspiration

I was nine years old when I pulled a book off the shelf from a library in Jackson, Michigan. As I opened the cover with a brown leathery finish, the aroma of the century-old book struck my senses like it was something undiscovered and bigger than life. The book's discolored pages felt soft and fragile, but the images sketched in it were defined and strong. I felt the pictures were calling my name. On one particular page there was an image of a mighty polar bear standing over a man with a spear. This drew me in with excitement. The man, who was clad in caribou fur clothing, had a look of terror in his eyes while the bear's eyes showed signs of ravage hunger. The most intriguing aspect of the image however was the large dog. He had massive broad shoulders and stood strong in front of the man protecting him from the ferocious bear.

Lost in a world of childish imagination, I visualized myself as the Inuit holding the spear while my beloved dog protected me.

As I carefully turned the book's pages, I became absorbed in its descriptions about a faraway frozen land where polar bears, wolves, and muskoxen thrived in a frozen wilderness. I wished I was there exploring this foreign and wild land. Yet, it wasn't the adventure of exploring that captivated me as much as it was the mysterious dog included in the stories and pictures.

This image, sketched by an unknown artist over a century ago, steered me to the course of life that I have taken. If it weren't for this inspiring book about the Arctic wilderness and the image of the man, bear, and dog, I would not be here today sharing my tales about the admirable dog breed represented in the pictures: the Alaskan malamute.

Blessed with a zest for adventure, I decided to follow my dream. I swore I wouldn't ever give up until I felt the cold frost of the Arctic air on my cheeks and the warm soft fur of a malamute in my palms. Now half a century later, I am here to tell you that everything I've read or suspected about the Arctic is true. It is a place where challenges, struggles, and adventures are waiting for those who dare to trespass into its realm. And the Alaskan malamute is alive and well, as this breed has been for several thousand years. Out of my love for these dogs and concern for preserving this dog breed, one of my goals in writing this book is to ensure that the traits of the malamute that are best for Arctic travel are appreciated, understood, and maintained for future generations of dog lovers and explorers like myself.

I admit there were times when I almost believed what I was told by others. Many times in the past and present, dog mushers told me that it's impossible to travel by dog team in regions of Alaska's Arctic where snow depth is over two or three feet deep. It was believed dogs cannot travel and pull heavy sleds in snow that is as deep as their necks unless they have a trail broken for them. However, after I devised a training strategy that specifically addresses breaking trail in extremely deep snow and designed a dog-hitch system that is more effective for freighting than the conventional dog-hitch system, I proved this myth to be wrong.

Deep snow and the Arctic's brutally harsh environment haven't been the only challenges I have faced. My entire life, I have been plagued with celiac disease, a genetic, autoimmune condition that prevents me from consuming gluten. For most of my life I wasn't aware of it and accepted that feeling ill was the norm.

After I learned of my disease and the fact that I was also lactose-intolerant, I was forced to follow a strict gluten-free and dairy-free diet that complicated Arctic travel. Extreme levels of activity like handling dogs that are 100 pounds or more, setting-up and breaking camp, snowshoeing, skiing, and surviving extreme cold temperatures require 8,000 to 10,000 calories a day. It's been a challenge to provide my body with proper nutrients and calories on a restricted diet. And for many years in the past, gluten-free food wasn't readily available like it is today. But after many failures, I've learned to overcome this handicap by adhering to a non-gluten, dairy-free calorie-dense diet. It requires more work to prepare and purchase food for a multi-month expedition, but I believe it's a blessing in disguise. The restricted diet has caused me to consume healthier foods, which I believe has resulted in a healthier life.

*Camped on the north side of Alaska's Brooks Range with a vast untouched
Arctic wilderness in the background yet to explore!*

Chapter 2: Beginning Expeditions

When I was five-years-old, my dad handed me a floppy-eared beagle that I named Prince. He and I were best friends for many years until one day he didn't come home after we had been hunting rabbits. Losing Prince devastated me. I loved and missed that happy-go-lucky dog. I felt like life wasn't the same without him; there was something missing. I had a dark empty void in my heart. Then one sunny, colorful day in autumn several years later, I decided to acquire another hunting dog, and then another and another. Eventually I had an assortment of hunting dogs including golden retrievers, Irish setters, hounds, and another beagle.

Now, a half century after my dad gave me Prince, I still have dogs. My dogs have been featured in movies, television commercials, documentaries, and have accompanied me on numerous Arctic expeditions. Of the many types of dogs I have had the opportunity to train and share my life with, Alaskan malamutes have been the most influential in how they have provided me with significant, life-changing experiences. These dogs have an uncanny way of getting inside your heart and capturing your trust and love. When they are by your side, it's like you are surrounded by your dearest family members and friends.

Twenty-two "happy-go-lucky" Alaskan malamutes doing what they love to do!.

When I moved to Alaska in the early 1980s, I found that sled dog racing dominated the dog mushing community. These racing teams consisted mostly of small, lean, and hyperactive dogs that had traits similar to hound dogs. I was told by several mushers that they were Alaskan huskies. I discovered there were only a few malamute freighting teams around. Mostly, malamutes were tethered to heavy chains beside homes in rural villages. It was a sad sight to see. Because I had read so many stories while growing up about Arctic exploration and seen so many old photos of large Alaskan malamutes, I was heartbroken to see them nearly nonexistent. It seemed like I arrived in Alaska at the end of the dogsled freighting and Arctic exploration era. The tough old-timers who had Alaskan malamutes for prospecting, exploration, and hauling supplies to goldmines and rural villages were a dying breed. And also dying was the knowledge of Arctic travel by dog team as well as an appreciation for the Alaskan malamutes' phenomenal intellect.

Alaskan malamutes are emotional, head-strong, loving, friendly, and intelligent. They are extremely loyal to those they trust and adore. But they lose their trust and love quickly if they get overworked or taken advantage of. Simply put, they take everything personally. If you don't know how to relate to them, it can be quite a challenge to train them.

I started dog mushing without any knowledge of how to do it whatsoever. No one had ever given me advice on how to get started. I just did it. However, I did have my childhood experience with hunting dogs and used that as the foundation of my training methods. I discovered at a very early age that all dogs are remarkably powerful, insomuch it's beyond human comprehension, yet only if they are allowed to exhibit their strength freely without threats of being overworked.

When I was 22, I moved to Alaska and worked for a hunting guide and then as a lumberjack in summer and spent the off-season, or winters, in the wilderness. One winter I lived in the Canadian wilderness; another I spent in the mountains west of Haines, Alaska. Then, one off-season, I decided I was going to head above the Arctic Circle, something I've always dreamed of doing. So I loaded my three sled dogs, a canoe, and six months of supplies into my old pickup truck and headed north with my girlfriend, who I had just met.

After driving for several days from Haines, Alaska, I found myself on the Dalton Highway, or Haul Road. At that time the Dalton Highway was also nicknamed the Kamikaze Trail because of its steep hills and hazardous sharp curves that led many inexperienced truck drivers to veer off the road and into the spruce trees. It is a dusty or muddy, bumpy, and twisted road that ends in the Prudhoe Bay oilfields. I remember my overloaded pickup truck accelerating nearly out of control down "Beaver Slide" that was one of the infamous heart-stopping hills on the highway.

After Beaver Slide and not long after I regained my composure and control of my truck, the thick muddy road led me up a steep hill. At the summit was an old weathered sign that read in big broad letters, ARCTIC CIRCLE. Right then and there, I knew I was almost home.

About 60 miles north of the Arctic Circle was an old-looking restaurant, a tire shop, a fuel station, and a post office named Coldfoot. Actually, the buildings weren't old but they certainly looked like it. The heavily painted shacks didn't hide the obvious scrap lumber used to build them. In those days, oil companies tossed old lumber in the dumps, or they left lumber unguarded. A few local residents happily helped themselves as if the whole lot of it was a glorious Christmas gift left by Santa. I'm sure a good portion of Coldfoot was built compliments of the oil companies' discarded and unguarded lumber.

After handing the Coldfoot's restaurant cashier a fist full of dollars for exorbitantly-priced gasoline, I turned the truck around and headed south on the highway. Earlier while driving north, I had spotted a winding crystalline river with tall spruce trees growing on its mossy banks. I figured trees similar to those would make fine cabin logs.

There was a small parking area by the river, so I parked the truck and offloaded our dogs and supplies into the canoe. After my girlfriend settled in place, there wasn't much room for me to sit, but I managed to squeeze in after I shoved us off into the swift current.

We paddled downriver until I saw a nice stand of spruce trees by a meadow along the shoreline. A birch tree in the center of the meadow had blanketed the grass with golden late-September leaves. It looked like a perfect site for a cabin. With an axe as my only tool, I built a small log cabin and we moved into it before the October snows began covering the forest floor a week later.

When freeze-up arrived in late October, I sewed three harnesses together with moose hide and built a sled from birch wood. That year was one of the coldest damn winters on record with temperatures plummeting to -65°F to -70°F. But I was so thankful and excited to be living in the far north that the frigid weather didn't hinder my enthusiasm to explore the sub-arctic wilderness whatsoever. I traveled everyday while exploring the river valleys with my three dogs. Sometimes my girlfriend joined me. Mostly though, she preferred to stay in the cozy cabin to bake bread and knit warm mitts and hats. I didn't blame her!

With such a small team, I never ever rode on the sled. The thought of riding on the sled never crossed my mind. It didn't make sense to me because I was fully capable of running, snowshoeing, or skiing ahead or behind the team. I couldn't wrap my head around the concept of standing on sled runners and asking my dogs that were already working hard to haul my ass around. It was this winter when I discovered the true strength of sled dogs and how to preserve that strength.

My girlfriend and I decided to return again and again to the Coldfoot area after the spring and summer logging seasons until we became permanent residences there several years later. However, I was new in the Coldfoot dog mushing community. For that reason, after my first season in the area, many local mushers including Iditarod champs kindly offered advice about training sled dogs.

Interestingly, I've found their training methods contradictory to mine. I believe that's mostly because they thought I wanted to race sled dogs and their training methods were specifically for racing. After all most dog mushers in the area raced dogs. So standing on the runners while the dogs were pulling was the norm for racing teams. But I wasn't interested in racing in the very least. I just wanted strong dogs that could break trail and pull lots of weight.

With subsequent seasons in Coldfoot and after my team grew in number, there were times when traveling beside the sled wasn't an option. When dogs are trotting on a groomed trail, their pace is faster than I can run so I'm forced to hop on the sled. Otherwise, I'd rather ski, walk, run, or snowshoe. However, as my team continually grows in strength, I still adhere to my dogsledding basics.

Additionally, I have modified many of the old methods. For example, my sleds are built of mostly lightweight plastic rather than heavy wood or steel. I've also devised methods and traveling strategies that aren't the norm. Significantly, I don't ever travel with a single sled regardless of the length of my trip. Aside from the U.S. mail teams prior to the 1940s, traveling with a single sled is still the standard. Additionally, my dog-hitch system is different from the conventional hitch systems both past and present. The harnesses I use, called the single tree harness, are the same design of a century ago except for a few modifications. Nowadays, they're identified by a different name but they are still the basic design that has been used for 100 years. You might say I'm a traditionalist because I'm still using many of the old-style methods and gear. But the truth is the old-style methods work best. Similar to the harnesses, my tent is an old design as well. When I built the tent I didn't realize it resembled Inupiat tents that were used for many centuries. I actually designed it without any knowledge of how Inupiat tents were made. I actually thought my tent was a one-of-a-kind design. Then one day while researching the Inupiat culture and people, who have resided in Alaska's Arctic for centuries, I found old photographs that were all dated 1907. To my surprise, these images showed Inupiat tents that looked exactly like mine. It became clear to me that this tent design was already in use for hundreds of years before I came on the scene.

After discovering the Inupiat tent design, I figured I'd replicate my clothing from the Inupiat as well. After all they live and thrive in the Arctic, whereas we non-natives freeze our butts off.

Our camp nestled in deep snow at the base of a mountain in the Brooks Range.

So, when fall arrived with a chill in the air and the caribou migrated across the treeless tundra, I harvested several healthy bulls and tanned their hides. I then carefully studied old photographs of Inupiat traditional winter clothing sewn of caribou fur and began sewing identical clothing for myself. After lots of screw-ups, broken needles, and sore fingers from sewing, I had a fine caribou fur parka, mitts, and several pairs of *mukluks* (boots). I couldn't wait to test out my new fur clothing in winter.

It wasn't long after I had finished sewing that winter swept across the barren landscape with a terrible vengeance and seemingly a hate for the living. I excitedly suited up with my Inupiat-inspired parka, mitts, and mukluks and faced the blowing fury of snow outside my cabin. I was shocked at how comfortable I was in -60°F wind chill. The caribou fur parka, mitts, and mukluks were far superior to the winter clothing sold in stores.

My first large malamute team of five was a mismatched assortment of dogs; misfits that other mushers didn't want. They were too slow or outright mean. Most mushers don't like slow dogs that can jeopardize a race or mean dogs that are hard to train. But these so-called mean dogs, I learned, were just lonely and starved for attention. With special care and love, my team of misfits became the friendliest and most behaved dog team around the Coldfoot area. They weren't fast and they could never compete with Alaskan huskies in races, but they could haul a heavy load and loved doing it.

With a team of five dogs, I finally had the ability to travel throughout the Brooks Range. Most of the time my homemade freight sled was heavily loaded so I spent my time on snowshoes busting trail in front of the leaders. That team of five dogs was tougher than hell. We broke trail, pitched camp, and explored the mountains. It was a time of freedom for me and them. The stars were my ceiling and the boreal forest was my home. My bed was a caribou hide spread out on the snow and a crackling campfire with the malamutes' howl as my music. Every night while the aroma of sweet wood smoke filled the air I watched the northern lights on the sky's stage.

Sometimes the lights flowed like ocean waves overhead in an array of colors and other times they danced and swirled in hazy greens. And one night they shot overhead as red as blood.

When the mercury sank to -60°F, the dogs weren't bothered at all. I adapted to the cold and was quite comfortable in my homemade caribou fur mukluks, mitts, and heavy parka.

I remember on one of my trips with the team I found myself standing on the Continental Divide viewing the Arctic's vast landscape. I was awestruck. The treeless wilderness looked desolate and brutally lonely, yet strangely inviting. The towering mountains stood torn and sharp above the rolling hills to the north. The immense white expanse struck a chord in me. It was like arriving home after a very, very long journey. And I knew my dogs felt the same way. My leader, Bruiser, who had one lazy ear, stared off in the expanse. This was where his ancestors originated; this was his homeland. Right then and there I vowed to Bruiser that we'd come back every winter. I knew the Arctic was where my heart was and I had to see and explore more of it. And I knew my dogs loved the place as much as I did. That said I knew that if I were to venture into the high Arctic I had to have dogs that could easily endure the climate. I knew my life and my survival depended on that fact. The dogs had to be well-trained, stout, healthy, and would have to meet the challenges of navigating on the open and windblown tundra as well as break trail in waist-deep snow.

The Alaskan malamute fit the criteria. Their strong survival instincts and intelligence far surpassed any other dog breed I had ever worked with. They had what it takes to live and thrive in the Arctic. To fulfill my dream to return each year, I knew deeply that I needed them. For that reason, I also knew I needed to develop a deep understanding of how to work and live with these beautiful animals, which I came to call cheerful warriors.

"Cheerful Warriors" breaking trail in four feet deep snow

Farmer is on the left with his son Junior while leading their

Chapter 3: Braving and Surviving the Challenges of Expeditions

The Allure of the Continental Divide

It was March 1985 and my team of five dogs and I were out exploring the rugged Brooks Range. I had two weeks of supplies in the sled when I left Nolan Creek and planned on turning around half-way, or a week, into our trip. As we traveled north, the jagged mountains with spiraled peaks cast shadows across the river we were traveling on. I was drawn to the rugged and raw beauty and felt compelled to go further up the river than I had planned. I figured on our return we could travel longer days since the sled would be lighter. Eventually, we found ourselves at the headwaters of the river with nowhere else to go except up a steep mountain pass. So, ignoring the fact that supplies were getting dangerously low, I climbed the pass with the dogs and our sled. Eventually, we found ourselves on the Continental Divide. I remember the view from where we stood like it was yesterday. Those wide-sweeping valleys, rolling hills, and endless miles of treeless terrain struck my soul. I vowed to my dogs we would return.

When I turned my team around that day on the Continental Divide, I calculated that I had four to five days of supplies and we were over one hundred miles from my cabin. Needless to say, I didn't waste any time on our return trip. I remember trotting in front of the team every day until the dark hours of the night, giving them encouragement and strength whenever their paces slowed down. Then I'd pitch camp directly on the trail and continue our marathon in the morning. Finally after the third day and night of

Most of Alaska's Arctic is a vast untouched wilderness, yet rarely traveled because of its deep snow and mountainous terrain.

17

traveling, I saw lantern lights glowing in my cabin's windows along Nolan Creek.

After this adventure, I realized a larger team was necessary for prolong trips into the Arctic. The fact that Alaskan malamutes require fewer calories per day to stay healthy compared to other dog breeds, including Alaskan huskies, I calculated a larger team could haul more dogfood, which would allow me to travel farther. This prompted me to search for additional purebred Alaskan malamutes for my team. But ironically, very few Alaskan malamute breeders were in Alaska. Most breeders were in the lower 48 (the continental U.S.) and the malamute puppies advertised were for the show ring or were from kennels that didn't work their dogs in the same manner that my team was worked. I didn't want to risk acquiring a bloodline that didn't have what it took for traveling in the Arctic.

I'm not saying other breeders' malamutes were lacking Arctic-compatible traits, but I understand that a working dog breed cannot retain its original physical characteristics unless the dogs are worked in a similar environment from which they originated. Drawing on my experience, I have found that a dog's weakness doesn't present itself unless he is worked. I figured many lower 48 breeders' dogs might have undesirable traits for my needs that they weren't aware of. And possibly they weren't familiar with traits that are important for Arctic travel as well.

Finally, one day in July, I met a fine clean-shaven gentleman named Roger who was overseeing work at his gold mine in Nolan Creek. He was dressed like the typical gold miner with sagging blue jeans held up by suspenders and wearing a soiled gray shirt and a faded blue baseball cap that shadowed the sun from his generous smile.

After a handshake and introducing ourselves, Roger and I seemed to relate to each other easily. I detected from shaking hands with him that he wasn't afraid of hard work. After a short discussion about falling gold prices and bureaucrats hindering mining operations with ridiculous regulations, we began talking about dog mushing and Alaskan malamutes. My interest elevated when Roger mentioned he hauled freight with a team of malamutes for the Denali National Park Rangers in 1971. Then I asked Roger where I could find some good solid malamutes for sale. Keeping his smile, he mentioned he had a few puppies he wanted to sell. I jumped at the opportunity and immediately agreed to purchase a puppy. We decided I would meet him at his home in Fairbanks after the summer gold mining season.

When October snows carpeted the jagged peaks that surrounded Nolan Creek, the prospectors closed the mines, gathered their gold, and headed south. I wasn't far behind them. I jumped in my pickup, filled the gas tank with fuel at Coldfoot, and headed down the dusty highway.

Roger was feeding his puppies when I drove my rattling old truck into his driveway. After quick greetings, I excitedly chose a beautiful black and white male puppy from the litter. Roger picked him up and set the fat furry butterball pup in my arms. "You will like this puppy," Roger said in deep baritone voice that always correlated with his smile. "I know I will, Roger," I responded and then added, "he certainly looks stout with those big paws."

I followed Roger inside his log home where coffee was simmering on the wood-burning stove. He poured some coffee into a mug and handed it to me. "Just move those papers aside on the table and have a seat," Roger said as he filled his own mug.

I noticed that the "papers" were government notices and addressed to his mining company. Apparently it was part of Roger's duty at his goldmine to stay up-to-date on regulations. I figured this explained his clean shaven face, whereas most miners were bearded.

"Before I forget," I said, "here's $250 for the pup." I reached into my pocket and pulled out the bills.

"Your pup is from a lineage of strong and hard workers," Roger said as he sat down at the table. He wrapped his hand around his mug and rested his elbows on the table. He continued, "When we were hauling supplies to Denali Park headquarters, his grandfather, Bandit, was one of my strongest pullers in the team. My partner, Tom, and I had thirteen dogs with over 1,500 pounds of supplies loaded in two sleds tied in tandem. It was a bastardly cold February afternoon when we left our base camp and before we knew it, it was dark. We knew the Healy Canyon was ahead of us but we had no choice but to continue."

Roger paused for a sip of coffee, settled back into his chair, focused his eyes on the squirming puppy in my arms, and continued, "That was a hair-raising experience, not knowing what was ahead of us in that canyon. It was dark, icy, and deathly silent except for the swishing sounds of the runners. We prayed there wasn't open water or thin ice ahead. We put our faith in our leader, Bobbie, too. He was from Kotzebue. What a great leader. He was feisty son-of-a-bitch, though. He lost his right ear in a fight later-on that trip." I gulped a big swallow of the strongest coffee I've ever had.

"We made it by the grace of God and arrived at Park headquarters at 8:00 p.m. Bandit pulled with all his heart that night. He inspired the team to keep going. He and Bobbie were real heroes." From the tone of Roger's voice, I detected true love for malamutes and wilderness adventure.

*****

As my team grew from five to twelve dogs, I found I could travel farther and stay longer in the Arctic. But staying longer in the Arctic wasn't always pleasant. Oftentimes the Arctic environment can be so damn brutally cold you would think nothing in God's great creation could survive it. Even though I've slept under the stars at -82°F and endured blistering cold windstorms in the southern Brooks Range, I've never experienced anyplace colder than Alaska's high Arctic. Hurricane force winds cut through clothing and can freeze your flesh in minutes. Eventually I became acclimated to the freezing temperatures and managed to live comfortably with only the bare necessities.

Alaskan malamutes are at home in the snow. This little fella is dreaming of joining his cousins on an Arctic expedition!

The most important necessity is an appropriate tent. After several years of suffering in so-called Arctic tents I had purchased in Fairbanks, I built the canvas tent described in the Chapter 2. This tent, based on a design used by the Inupiat, could withstand strong winds and accommodate a small wood-burning stove. In addition to helping the tent stay warm, the wood heat allowed me to dry my clothes and that eliminated the constant threat of hyperthermia. But firewood is scarce, since trees are rare in the Arctic. Fortunately, I discovered that the willow brush alongside creeks and rivers burned well in my stove, providing it was dry.

Staying dry and warm weren't the only challenges, however. The most challenging aspect about traveling in Alaska's Arctic is breaking trail through deep snow, sometimes five to six feet deep. I remember being told by many old timers and dog mushers that it isn't possible for dogs to travel in snow over two feet deep. But I never wanted to believe them. If I did, my dream of exploring Alaska's Arctic with a dog team was over. Like myself, I didn't believe my dogs were limited in what they could accomplish if they put their hearts into it and we were prepared to overcome obstacles.

Drawing upon my experiences with struggles in the Canadian wilderness before I arrived in Alaska, I learned strength is drawn from within you. It's this inner strength that motivates people to accomplish amazing and incredible things. I've discovered from training dogs for many years that they have an inner strength as well and are stronger than we realize. After a few years of working (and mostly struggling) with my dogs in the Arctic, I created a training strategy that draws out the amazing strengths and desires of malamutes. It's a training strategy that has resulted in my dogs accomplishing the "impossible." One of the many expeditions that my team of Alaskan malamutes has successfully accomplished, which highlights their incredible strengths, was the Leffingwell Expedition.

Farmer is on the left with Junior leading their teammates through deep snow.

During the winters of 2006–2008, my team and I conducted a series of unprecedented, multi-month solo expeditions in Alaska's Arctic Brooks Range and the Arctic National Wildlife Refuge (ANWR). Pulling three sleds in tandem with two tons of supplies, the team and I mushed entirely without resupply for up to four months without seeing another human being. The expedition or the Leffingwell Expedition was a tribute to the forgotten explorer Ernest de Koven Leffingwell (1876-1971).

Leffingwell was a member of the Anglo-American Polar Expedition (1906-1908) that established that

21

there was no land north of Alaska. Leffingwell, along with other members of the expedition, became stranded on the Arctic Ocean coastline. Their ship, *Duchess of Bedford*, became ice-locked and unseaworthy, so the men used the wood from the ship to build a cabin. For the next eight years (1906 to 1914), Leffingwell stayed there to conduct his successful mapping project. He is credited with mapping much of the Arctic coast and the Brooks Range, which is now part of ANWR.

To do his work, Leffingwell traveled by dog team to cover ground in winter and used a small boat to follow the coastline during summer months. Traveling with his journals and maps as a guide, the dogs and I covered much of the same country, camped in many of the same locations that Leffingwell had a century before.

Since the Leffingwell Expedition, I have conducted a dozen multi-month expeditions, all of which were unassisted (without resupply) including a 100-day solo in 2013 and multiple expeditions lasting up to three months. These expeditions are unprecedented in modern-day Arctic exploration and never in recorded history has anyone traveled solo with a team of 22 malamutes for multiple months in one of the most brutal environments on Earth without resupply, or even so much as seeing another person. I attribute the success of the expeditions entirely to the Alaskan malamutes. They are a one-of-a kind breed and unmatched by any other when it comes to stamina.

A dog's iron will and a person's spirit combined is a formidable force. They become one team, one being, one cohesive unit working together to overcome what was believed to be impossible.

--From my book, *The Malamute Man: The Brute Force of Unified Souls* (2017)

This photo shows Farmer and Junior happily working with their teammates as one cohesive unit.

Chapter 4: Through the Eyes of a Malamute

There's an instinctive allure for many of us to have dogs in our lives. Dogs have been with humankind for many thousands of years and perhaps our deep feeling toward these dependable animals is driven by ancient DNA when many populaces' lives relied on dogs for protection and companionship.

Often we look for answers to our questions in books and magazines. Yet, regardless of what we read, we discover that we learn best from our experiences. Our psychological capacity to learn through direct experience is more meaningful, effective, and efficient than reading about them. The same goes with learning how to train dogs. We must experience the scenario before we can fully comprehend how to react or act while training our pups.

I have found that another effective tool is to practice visualizing life from a dog's perspective. This book won't give you the direct experience of being out on the snow and ice with your animals, but reading it will give you guidance in getting in touch with a dog's brain and point of view so that you can practice experiencing the world through his or her eyes.

The Story of Boss: A Cheerful Warrior

Inside Boss's canine cranium a glorious plan was conceived. One day she would become the lead dog. Her dream seemed far-fetched though. How could a runt who weighed only 60 pounds be capable of leading a team of 22 hardened Alaskan malamutes that were twice her size? I am here to tell you her story and how she accomplished this impossible goal with nothing more than a fearless heart and a cheerful warrior demeanor.

There is one small quirk about Boss I should tell you about first. Boss had a menacing side of her personality, and I am sure you know someone in your circle of friends or family that has a similar personality trait. Even though Boss succeeded in obtaining the most prestigious status of the team she wasn't entirely satisfied. Boss was driven and determined to serve justice on all those who bullied her when she was young, including Sally. Boss hated Sally with perfect passion.

When Boss was born she didn't have a fighting chance in hell to survive. She was the only pup of the litter, or a "singleton." It's rare for a malamute to have only one puppy, but it happens nonetheless. Usually the single puppy is large, vibrant, and healthy at birth. But this wasn't the case with Boss. She was small and frail. To make matters worse, her mother, Sheba, a beautiful grey and white gal who loved to hog my cot, didn't want Boss near her and often pushed Boss out of the warm bed of straw. Sheba wasn't interested in keeping the newborn alive.

Once in a while though, Sheba showed a spark of compassion and nursed her. Mostly though, she would turn her back on Boss. It seemed Sheba wanted the little girl as any mother wants their offspring with the strongest love and compassion that is known, yet I believe Sheba might have noticed Boss was physically inferior. It just didn't make sense to try to keep a weak pup alive. Sheba was influenced, beyond her control, by ancient instincts to allow the sweet little Boss to die in order to serve the greater benefit of preserving the pack's strength and longevity.

But, I had no such ancient loyalty. So, every day I bottle-fed the little grey fur ball regular milk to supplement whatever she was getting from Sheba. I looked forward to watching Boss suckle on the bottle, grunting and seemingly smiling as the warm milk dripped off tiny hairs on her chin. Boss and I grew together.

As time passed, Sheba became more detached from Boss. Then one day I found Boss several feet away from her whelping pen while Sheba lay inside curled up with her eyes tightly closed. Sheba had decided it was time to let Boss go.

Immediately, I picked up the helpless puppy and held her muzzle to my ear. I could smell the sweet puppy smell of Boss but she wasn't breathing. I felt like part of me died inside. I held her under my shirt hoping to warm her. My heart sank with pain as I felt her cold lifeless limbs against my belly. "C'mon, girl, you can make it," I whispered, hoping for a miracle.

I rushed inside my tent, a wooden frame with a fabric roof, and held her above the heat that radiated from the hot wood-burning stove. As I massaged her tiny heart and lightly squeezed and "pumped" her lungs, I hoped and prayed to detect a heartbeat, but I felt nothing. As she lay in the palm of my hand, with her eyes closed and her head hanging, I reminisced how a day earlier she was full of life and joy.

Now, losing her was a reality. But I couldn't and wouldn't give up. I continued to massage her heart and pump her lungs. As the crackling flames slowly died to a dark whisper in the stove and one of my tears sizzled on the stove's surface, I accepted the fact that Boss would never be in my team. She would rest peacefully for the rest of time. Maybe, I thought, I'd bury her on a hilltop where the vast Arctic openness could be viewed on all sides.

Then, suddenly and unbelievably, she coughed, inhaled a short breath and whined a sweet tune of life and desperation. My heart jumped as my fingertips felt Boss's tiny racing heart through her fragile ribs.

When I was assured she could breathe on her own, I set her on a soft caribou hide and fed her warm milk. As I watched Boss's feistiness return, I realized she was going to be a very, very special girl.

As Boss slowly grew from a fragile helpless puppy that slept in the palm of my hand to an adolescent that hogged the cot, I knew she wasn't going to be large. Even though she was proportional with thick bones, paws, and a wide chest, she was much smaller than any malamute I've ever had the pleasure of having.

One day, Boss was inside the cabin where I had leaned a small mirror against the wall to repair the hinge that it hung on. Boss, with her curious nature, rushed where I stood and caught a glimpse of her reflection in the mirror. Almond eyes stared back at her and she jumped in fear and bewilderment.

Then, Boss showed her glistening white canines, poised to attack the other grey girl that mimicked her. Suddenly, Boss surprised the heck out of me; she cut-loose the ugliest and most atrocious growl that I've ever heard come from the throat of a malamute. Her deep guttural growl would have scared the crap out of the wickedest grizzly bear in the Arctic. I busted out laughing, which scared Boss and sent her scampering under the table, leaving claw marks scribed in the plywood floor.

After Boss regained her composure, she glanced at me, and then crept out from under the table to approach her adversary again. Her beautiful grey hackles stood tall like porcupine quills while she worked her large furry paws toward the mirror. She wasn't going to let that girl in the mirror get the best of her. She was going back to settle the score. As Boss slowly stepped closer to the mirror, she inhaled deeply, and then exhaled with a threatening growl. She raked her eyes up and down, evaluating her enemy in the steamed-up mirror. Boss's enemy did the same. Boss turned her head and looked at me for assurance. I smiled and nodded. Boss's tense muscles relaxed and she sat down mesmerized at the beautiful malamute that was in front of her.

Boss sat there for a few moments. Then, she stood up, stretched out like a cat, sniffed the mirror again, turned around, and proudly walked away with her tailed curved tightly over her back. As she walked away, I swear she strutted a little. Right then and there, I knew Boss had decided that she was a badass and the most beautiful Alaskan malamute in the world. This is when I decided to name her Boss.

A few months later . . .

As the blood-red sun led my eyes to the snowy hills on the horizon in late November, Boss pranced beside the gang line of 22 malamutes hitched to three enormous freight sleds. Like a drill sergeant, Boss loved antagonizing them.

If she could speak, I bet she would be saying: "Alright, soldiers. Listen-up. We're going to bust trail through one of the most God-awful brutal places on Earth. If you aren't ready, you better damn well get ready right now! We aren't coming back until the snow is melted and the rivers are flowing—five months from now. So buck it up! Especially you, Sally! Damn you, girl—stand tall. Don't be a slouch!"

It was late November and I had been training by running nearby trails multiple times per day for three months for this particular expedition called the Leffingwell Expedition and was fit as an Olympic athlete and so were the dogs. And it had been a month since the last plane had dropped off supplies and we had seen another person. It was just me, Boss, and the team in the middle of Alaska's Arctic.

During the expedition, I didn't have communication with the outside world unless I dragged an antenna to a hilltop and dialed from my first generation (analog) mobile phone. It was heavy and setting up the equipment to get a signal was such a pain, I only checked in with family and friends once in a while. If the country began fighting World War III, I wouldn't have known it. Honestly, the only thing I was concerned about was the dogs' safety and mine in one of the most inhospitable environments in the world.

From late November to May we fought through blinding blizzards, -90°F wind chills, waist deep snow, and 72 days without seeing the glistening golden rays of the sun. We had dropped through thin ice; fallen into a mountain crevasse, which resulted in me having broken ribs; and fended off a charging grizzly bear. But none of these hardships mattered because Boss and the team were at my side. I relied on my team for survival as much as they depended on me for their survival.

We were one team, one cohesive unit that lived, traveled, endured trials, and celebrated triumphs together. I wasn't ever an alpha figure; I was just a team member and coach. I encouraged them through tough times and they inspired me when I was exhausted and depleted of energy.

Essentially, I mimicked my malamutes' strengths, hardiness, and cheerful warrior demeanors. Without them as my mentors, I could not have ever held up to the extreme struggles and physical demands of breaking trail across Alaska's Arctic Brooks Range for several months on end.

When people and dogs endure hardships, an unbreakable bond is created. It's a bond that lasts for a lifetime.

When both an animal and a person recognize that their survival depends on each other, there is no longer a dominate role for either the person or animal. They work and live together as one unit. Emotions are felt between them like they are one being—when one suffers or feels joy so does the other.

Regardless of the many struggles we faced, I saw amazing Arctic landscapes that are rarely viewed by humans in winter. The team and I busted trail where it was believed to be impossible to travel by dog team.

We explored jagged canyons that cut deep into the flesh of mountains with peaks that scraped the clouds, and we summited passes over the Continental Divide. On many nights, the northern lights dashed overhead in magnificent displays of greens, reds, and purple colors, illuminating our tranquil surroundings. If you were there, you'd think it was like living under an enormous glass window while a painter's brush worked colorful ocean wave designs on the other side of the glass. All-in-all I felt humbled to be in the presence of such a glorious sky and a landscape that was carved, molded, and shaped by our Creator's mighty hand.

On Christmas day, I camped alongside some "warm" springs. The springs weren't warm enough to take a dip, but it was awfully more convenient for brewing coffee than having to melt snow.

While I was scooping a coffee pot of crystalline spring water, a little red fox trotted across the snowy tundra and circled the malamutes on the picket line. The little guy had been following us for about two weeks and scavenged morsels of dogfood left in the snow after we struck camp.

Now, Fox apparently felt comfortable visiting us. And he seemed to enjoy teasing the dogs. But, big bad Boss decided to put a stop to that. She charged Fox, sending him running for his life. But, then he stopped dead in his tracks, swung around, and faced Boss nose-to-nose. Boss seemed to relish the challenge and didn't back down. Then her bushy tail swirled around in circles similar to what a male malamute does when he meets a girlfriend.

After a short moment, little Fox darted around Boss like his tail was on fire. Boss reacted by immediately chasing the wild little red flash of fur that circled her until she nearly bit his tail. Fox stopped in his

27

tracks and then they squared off again and they repeated their circus show.

Boss and Fox played for about two to three minutes, and then he turned tail and trotted across an ice bridge over the warm springs and disappeared into the tall willows at the opposite side of the river. Boss just sat on her haunches panting and watching him go.

Boss was only 10-months-old at this time and wasn't mature enough to pull in the team. As I have said, I never allow my dogs pull anything until they're at least two years old. So during this particular expedition Boss just tagged-along beside the sled or rode in it.

Sometimes, Boss would get a little bored and feel it was her responsibility to irritate Sally who was in the wheel position (with the dogs closest to the sled). Sally was a beautiful red gal with a stocky build who enjoyed pulling beside her big brothers, Nikko and Farmer. But she had a chip on her shoulder with Boss.

Boss in lead on the right with Bear and Farmer

Sally was the only girl in her litter, so she was accustomed to dominating her brothers and she didn't like any other dog challenging her. All the other girls approached Sally with submission, grace, and respect, except Boss.

Fast forward to a few years later, Boss was over three and half years old when I slipped a small harness on and attached her tug line. She worked well in the team and advanced quickly up the ranks from wheel to swing position. So, I decided to place her in lead after we traveled north of the mountains to the Beaufort Sea in late April. During this time the rivers in the mountains began running so we usually traveled on the sea ice where it was solidly frozen and free of water. I just figured it would be less stressful for her on the sea's hard pack snow.

Finally her big day arrived and we trotted off the snowy tundra and onto the sea ice. After the team settled into a comfortable trot I placed Boss in lead beside my "sea ice" leader Bear, who I used exclusively on the sea because he was much smaller than his teammates and preferred a faster trot. Like

28

an opening act in a grand parade down Main Street, Boss led the team magnificently for an entire day. But unbeknownst to me, it was just a staged act. Boss had a plan and wanted to settle an old score. She probably figured the lead position was a prime opportunity to do so and took full advantage of it.

While trotting on a smooth area of the sea ice Boss managed to turn the entire team of 22 dogs around, dragging Bear along with her, and go after Sally. As fur flew and growls thundered across the ice I dove in the midst of the brawl and pulled Boss away from her rival. I spent the following hour straightening out the team that was tied in a perfect 22-dog tangled knot. I swear Boss was smiling ear-to-ear the rest of the evening. Not only had she accomplished the impossible by becoming a lead dog for a team of toughened malamute freighters, she somehow managed to even the score with a gal who picked on her when she was young.

Thereafter, Sally and Boss were best of friends, except once in a while when they'd offer each other an evil look and growl, but all-in-all they were best buds.

Of the many adventures and Arctic expeditions that I have shared with my malamutes for the past 35 years, I believe this 2013 Arctic expedition was one of the most memorable. It was a 100-day solo that led me and the team of Alaskan malamutes deep into the mighty Brooks Range of Alaska.

The photos in this book were taken during this tough expedition. From January to April, snow was waist- to chest-deep and everyday was a struggle. Despite the unprecedented snowfall that winter, the malamutes remained happy and strong. It was a true testament to their cheerful warrior demeanor. Their cheerful warrior trait has always fascinated me. And it has mystified me. Where did this trait come from? How and why?

It wasn't until I researched the history of these magnificent dogs and experienced the environment in which they originated did I begin to understand how their minds work and the significance of their cheerful demeanors. It so happens to be the most precious survival trait they possess.

Boss is in the center of my seven wheel dogs "learning the ropes" during an expedition along the coast of Alaska's Arctic

Boss on the left posing for the photo

LEADERS

TEAM DOGS

SWING DOGS

WHEEL DOGS

Chapter 5: Young Malamutes (Before Physical Training Begins) and a Brief History of Malamutes

The strength of an Alaskan malamute is hidden in its heart. And it will remain hidden unless otherwise allowed to exhibit itself without fear. Let me explain. Inside the mind of a malamute is a complex world of ancient survival instincts and modern day conditioning from our society. Malamutes are an ancient domesticated dog breed and their origins quite possibly are associated with the Paleo-Indians who crossed the Bering Land Bridge to Northern Alaska 18,000 years ago.

In ancient times, malamutes were most likely used as pack animals.

And it's believed they were used to protect children and families from large, common predators at the time, while the adults were away hunting and gathering. So, malamutes have an ingrained love and respect for people and children. And they will do anything to please the people they adore. But, if they do not trust or adore the person they are with, they will simply draw upon their survival instincts and hold back their incredible strengths. And this mediocre strength pattern eventually carves a "deep groove" into their brain's neural pathway.

Once a certain behavior pattern becomes the default it requires lots of work to change it. So, this is the reasoning behind my previous comments that training malamutes should be mostly psychological rather than physical. That said, light exercise when they are young (and before dogsled training begins around the time they are two years old) enables their muscles and bodies grow into strong adults. But this doesn't mean working them in harness or running beside a team or pulling tires around the yard. I prefer to think of them as 6 to 8 year-old children. They run and play at their own pace and rest when they want.

Young malamutes need to play in a positive way. It's up to us to guide them in this play and to provide an environment for it so that they develop the right "groove" in their brains. Malamutes thrive when their lives are positive. They need to grow and develop in positive environments around positive people. If you provide these elements for them, they will end up being well-trained and happy and, whatever happens, your dog will be smiling always like a cheerful warrior.

Remember though, dogs can smell 100,000 times better than us so they can also smell our neural transmitters (as I mentioned in the Introduction). They can tell how you are feeling, whether you're angry, stressed, or happy. And their demeanors will reflect your emotions. Just keep that in mind as you're training your pup.

There is another point worth mentioning: Malamutes do not perform well out of fear. They perform to please. They do not view people as their peers. They instinctively look up to people and adore us. If they want to please us, they will do so with all their strength.

In contrast, correcting them with alpha dog gestures destroys this love and respect for us. If we want our malamutes to perform to their highest potential then I recommend staying clear of this training method.

One of my goals in writing this book series is to help the Alaskan malamute be better understood. I want to share my training techniques to help those who own these dogs. I hope that owners who learn my techniques will better understand and appreciate their dogs so that these beautiful animals are far less likely to be mishandled and end up in rescue shelters.

Although physical dogsled training begins around two years old, psychological training begins when puppies open their tiny eyes for the first time and view the big wide world around them. From this point forward, their natural mental strengths are nurtured, preserved, and prepared for their future. In my case, their future is the possibility of becoming a sled dog, in particular, a freighter and trail breaker.

Before we dive into the specifics of my training strategy, let's look into Alaskan malamutes' history.

Inside a malamute's mind are ancient and mysterious traits, behavior patterns, and survival instincts we know very little about. But we do know they are capable of exhibiting strength beyond human comprehension.

The question is where did this strength come from? And more importantly, how do we preserve it?

As you look into the dark almond eyes of your malamute who might be sitting on the couch and nibbling on kernels of buttered popcorn (a favorite treat for malamutes) while your kids are tugging on his tail, it's difficult to fathom that this magnificent breed goes back thousands of years to when they battled bears and other large predators.

When the first Paleo-Indians crossed the grassy plains of Beringia, or the Bering Land Bridge, around 18,000 years ago they settled in a vast region of rolling hills, plateaus, and wide sweeping rivers.

Nowadays, this region in Alaska's Arctic is called the Brooks Range Foothills. Evidence discovered near the Colville River in this region suggests dogs accompanied these hardy Paleo-Indian souls who migrated across the land bridge.

Whether or not these particular dogs were the original Alaskan malamutes is not known for sure. But we are certain that Alaskan malamutes are an ancient dog breed. According to recent DNA studies there are markers that can be traced to Tibetan wolves which prove their origins are from Asia. So the possibility the Paleo-Indians traveled with malamutes exists.

Originally, however, it's believed malamutes were used as pack animals rather than sled dogs. Also, they probably provided protection for families from bears and other large animals that were in the region.

I'm sure life for malamutes in ancient times was brutally tough. Deep within their beings and DNA are thousands of years of adaptations to harsh climates, starvation, struggles, and hardships. Yet it required intelligence, perseverance, stubbornness, and an inner strength that knows no bounds to have had endured ancient life.

This high level of strength was required to survive during this ancient age. The environment was much like it is today in Alaska's Arctic: hurricane force winds with -70°F to -90°F wind chills, blinding blizzards, deep snow, and mid-winter torrential downpours were many of Mother Nature's arsenal of weapons.

And similar to today, there were high winds that commonly scoured the treeless landscape and shaved off low lying willow brush like a sharp machete. The dogs in ancient times had to endure these vicious winds and conditions without shelter.

In summer, the struggles were of a different sort. The dogs had to utilize their fortitude, or inner strength, to endure the hardships associated with 24-hour sunlight that sometimes exceeded 80°F degrees. They were tortured with hordes of mosquitoes that took no mercy on exposed flesh. Their eyes and muzzles were constantly attacked from these merciless blood-suckers, but luckily, they could find relief by covering their muzzles with their brushy tails. And as in the winter, the dogs suffered without shelter.

In ancient times, malamutes would have been required to carry heavy packs of meat and supplies for the families that cared for them. Sometimes, however, when families didn't have enough game meat to feed their dogs, they hauled them by means of skin boats, or *umiaks*, to islands in the sea, abandoning them there to fend for themselves.

Occasionally, though, when the families acquired abundant supplies of meat, they brought portions of the meat to the islands where the dogs were. In fall, when snow blanketed the tundra and the ponds began to ice over they retrieved the survivors and prepared for their annual migration to the mountains, or Brooks Range.

When I was invited for dinner by an elderly woman from an Alaskan village, she told me an interesting fact that I hadn't ever heard before. As the elder busied herself preparing dinner, she stared outside the window at my dog team bedded in the snow. A moment later, she turned to me with a tear rolling off her dark weathered cheek, set a dish of sliced raw muktuk on the table and said in an ancient tone, "Long ago, each family here had around three dogs. Our dogs looked like some of yours, big and wide. We loved them. Those dogs were our family. I was only this high when dad let me ride on the sled."

She said this as she raised her hand beside the table where a bowl of Dall sheep soup simmered for her husband who was deaf. She continued, "I remember like it was yesterday. We were lost in a terrible blizzard. Dad picked me and my sister up, set us on the sled, and let the dogs lead the way through the snowstorm while he trotted behind us. The dogs led us home. They saved us. God, I miss those dogs now."

Three dogs is a very small team. Those dogs had to have been tough as nails and stronger than hell, because traveling by dog team in Alaska's Arctic, particularly in deep snow just north of the Brooks Range isn't an easy feat for a small team.

Whether you travel to Alaska's inland from Kotzebue, up the Kobuk River, or travel from the Beaufort Sea to the Brooks Range, the snow is deep and traveling is brutally slow. In the early days, the native peoples of Arctic Alaska migrated inland, toward the mountains, every winter and returned to the coast in spring, with exception of Barrow, where it's believed to have been the only permanent village in Alaska's Arctic.

From the information I have gathered, the father of the family usually walked ahead of the team and broke trail, while the rest of the family helped the dogs either by pushing or pulling the sled. If the family had an infant, he or she rode on the sled.

The sleds were extraordinarily heavy and were loaded with several hundred pounds of supplies and gear for the family to survive the winter in the mountains. The mountains, or Brooks Range, provided refuge from the perpetual coastal winds and offered populations of Dall sheep, moose, and caribou to harvest.

I've travelled extensively throughout Alaska's Arctic including the coastal regions and the Brooks Range for 35 years and have found the Brooks Range is a "paradise" in comparison to the sea coast during the dead of winter. But the Brooks Range is very diverse in terrain, wind, and weather.

Often, I've dog mushed in the upper Brooks Range elevations where snow was chest deep and have found adjacent valleys that were windswept with only knee-deep snow. Many of these areas are where some Arctic natives lived in the past.

During the 100-day 2013 Arctic expedition I never saw any humans or signs of human activity whatsoever. It's truly an untouched Arctic wilderness. And this region of the Brooks Range was considered inaccessible by dogteam because of its deep snow and and steep terrain. But Alaskan malamutes have proven this belief otherwise

Interestingly though, I haven't ever found evidence of ancient native people residing in valleys where snow can be chest deep. Most likely the natives didn't occupy the extreme deep snow areas because game populations avoided these areas as well. But I have found plenty of evidence of ancient people living in areas where snow was knee to waist deep. Usually evidence of ancient people can be found on high ridges that are windswept of snow that are common in nearly all the valleys in the Brooks Range. The main evidence that I search for and have discovered is in the form of tent rings. Tent rings are a circular distribution of heavy stones that were used to anchor tents from high winds. I also have found caches that were used to protect game meat from birds and foxes. These caches look like rectangular boxes and are entirely built of stones.

Areas with extremely strong wind were also avoided. A perpetual strong wind makes hunting, especially with bows and arrows and spears, virtually impossible. I remember one particular story about a family who never returned when they ventured into a windy region that most native people avoided. After this region was described to me, I recognized it in my travels.

I have been through this region a dozen times and it's certainly a vicious wind tunnel. The valley lies east to west whereas most valleys in Alaska's Arctic run north and south. Predominately west winds excel in velocity through this particular wide valley that eventually narrows like a bottle neck causing the wind to compress and further increase in speed. But caribou thrive here because it's windswept of snow and has exposed grasses that flourish in the mineral-rich soil.

For humans to live in this area, however, where the wind often exceeds hurricane forces with minus -90°F to -100°F wind chill temperatures, a high volume of high-calorie food would be required. Myself, I'll consume 10,000 calories a day when it is minus -80°F to -90°F. In order for an entire family with dogs to survive, an exceptionally large amount of rich meats and fats would be needed, and caribou, which are relatively lean in winter, would not be a sufficient food source.

So if a person didn't have large intakes of fats, like sheep mutton to digest in addition to lean caribou meat, he or she would eventually starve. I believe this is why most families resided deep in the Brooks Range during winter because they weren't tormented by cold winds and because sheep and caribou were plentiful.

Earlier I mentioned Barrow where people lived in a permanent village, but here they relied on a marine mammal diet rather than strictly caribou and sheep. And their dogs didn't have to be large and broad because they weren't required to break trail through waist-deep snow. This possibly might be why there is such a variation in the size of Alaskan malamutes.

This chapter just gives a glimpse into the Alaskan malamutes' past and how they have evolved into such powerfully-built dogs.

Breaking trail comes natural to Alaskan malamutes.

The team patiently waiting for my return from scouting a route across a small canyon not shown in photo.

Chapter 6: Nurturing Your Puppy

Since your puppy's brain and overall physical stature doesn't mature until at least two years old and actually doesn't fully mature until four to five years old, it's important to allow them to develop and grow at their own pace.

Myself, I prefer to envision how life might be like through the eyes of dogs. I believe doing this helps me understand them better.

Hopefully, the following story paints a picture or describes my "training" (or nurturing) strategy with puppies. The story takes place at my previous home in Alaska's Arctic.

Puppies learning to break trail and loving it

Three Pups: Farmer, Nikko, and Sally

When the midnight sun's golden spears bled through the partially opened door of the whelping box, Farmer pulled quickly away from his mother's warm tummy.

His inner being craved to be near the light, to touch and feel it. He had noticed the light before, yet now it seemed to be calling him. Beyond the light shining through, he saw a wonderful scene with tall grasses bowing in the wind. It was unlike the small enclosed world that he had known until now. Beyond the grasses, he saw an endless expanse of low rolling hills, meadows, and small stands of willow. Even though Farmer wasn't familiar with the strange world that revealed itself, he was struck with desire to explore it.

When Farmer moved hastily toward the light, every step through the straw felt like a giant leap. His adrenaline flowed swiftly through his veins while his heart raced and pounded quickly inside his deep chest.

Now getting closer, he smelled the sweet aromas from the Arctic's flora and heard songs of chickadees in the grasses. The scents and sounds awakened his senses and excited his inner being. But torn between his mother's loving bond and a yearning to explore, he stopped for a moment to ponder his quest. He turned and glanced at his mother, Ginger, a beautiful grey-colored gal comfortably lying on the soft bed of straw. She was watching him. He felt the light on his broad shoulders and noted earthly scents before him. Fighting against his instincts to stay with his Ginger; he turned away and continued on his quest.

As he stepped over his brother, Nikko, who was sleeping, he was met by Sally, his sister. Sally stepped aside and followed him with her eyes. She wanted so much to join him. Yet leaving the warmth and security of her mother and her nourishing milk was too much for her to take.

She noticed how Farmer's fluffy coat matched the color of the bronze light outside and wondered if she was as beautifully cloaked in fur as he.

Farmer reached the light that seeped through the door and felt the rays of warmth penetrate his thick fur. He pressed his muzzle against the door and surprisingly the door swung joyously open. It was like a curtain unveiling a magnificent world.

Like a puppy diving into a lake for the first time, Farmer jumped forward. As Sally watched him disappear, she turned, stepped over Nikko's head on her way to cuddle close to Ginger, and began nursing. Nikko softly growled, rolled over, and then waddled toward Ginger to join Sally.

Outside the whelping pen, Farmer's eyes widened with excitement. The tall grasses waved at him in the wind, enticing him to explore further into the creation of liveliness and openness. The sounds of ducks splashing in a nearby pond sparked his curiosity. The sweet smells of wildflowers captured his senses. As he dashed through the grasses only his brushy tail was visible. He was filled with joy and became lost in a world of beauty, light, and fresh earthly scents.

Suddenly he stopped. His sagging ears twitched at the faint sounds of Ginger's whimper. He listened closely, but the sounds had gone away. He only heard his panting and how it chimed with the breeze. Then, the mournful cries of his mother reached his ears again. He turned around and dashed toward the pen—or so he thought.

He was lost. The tall grasses that had seemed friendly were now his enemies and they fiercely blocked his flight. He wanted so much to be with his mother, to feel her warmth and caressing tongue, because now the golden light and earthly scents were too much and didn't feel safe.

Ginger's mournful howl shook his inner being. His bond for her was as strong as tempered steel. It could not be broken. He focused his senses to follow the whimpers of Ginger and ran as fast as he could but he felt his short legs couldn't move fast enough. He cried and whimpered in agonizing fear.

Finally, Farmer arrived at the pen's entrance. It felt like it had taken an eternity. Gathering his strength, he inhaled a deep breath, pushed open the swinging door with his muzzle, and stepped into the darkness. He then scampered quickly to his mother, shoved his muzzle next to Sally's and latched on Ginger's teat. Ginger caressed him as he shook with fright. Now, as the soothing warm sweet milk flowed down his throat, he thought he wanted never again to leave his mother or siblings. But those thoughts would soon dissipate.

As Farmer grew from a stocky, five-week-old puppy to a two-month-old handsome boy whose body was quickly changing into an adolescent, he became more daring and adventurous. Nikko and Sally, also growing up just as fast, joined him on his adventures.

Farmer enjoyed a typical puppy life of carefree playing in the grasses, chasing ducks, and exploring the wonderful world around him. He relished digging in the tundra and cherished the sensation of being covered in soil and smelling like a tussock. His greatest joys, however, were inside the cabin. It was there, where a gentle hand offered him delicious morsels of flavorful popcorn. Farmer relished the sounds of popcorn popping in the cast iron kettle as much as he savored each and every kernel handed to him.

This being, or person, who gave him treats and such comfort and contentment meant the world to him. He looked up to him like a friend and loved him unconditionally. He sensed and felt these feelings were mutual. Yet, Farmer was still very much connected to his mother who had provided rich nourishment and caressed him as a newborn.

Oftentimes, Farmer would lead Nikko and Sally to the kennel where their mother lived. When they trotted toward her, her almond eyes widened with excitement and love. For now, there was a bond, but soon Farmer and his siblings would go through dramatic changes in their brains and physical development that would lead to the mutual attachment with Ginger being significantly less special and marked by tail-wagging happiness.

Now, it was mid-August and the summer's bashing heat was gone as well as the hordes of mosquitoes that tortured them. Instead, there were vicious black flies that bit Farmer and his siblings mercilessly. He learned from watching Ginger to protect himself from the black flies by curling up with his brushy tail over his eyes and muzzle. This worked well with mosquitoes, too, and Farmer would utilize this defense posture to protect himself from blizzards that would soon sweep across the treeless landscape.

As the golden willow leaves drifted to the ground and the air was fresh and crisp, Farmer and his siblings became more vigorous and rambunctious than ever before. They sensed something exciting was going to happen. The person, who they so much adored, was now busy moving about with a sense of urgency.

A month later, as the glowing green northern lights illuminated the sky's black canvas, Farmer felt the chill of September penetrate his fur. During the day, ducks were no longer swimming about in the ponds and the soft blades of grass that Farmer enjoyed playing in, felt dry, crunchy, and lifeless.

Then one day, a fluffy white substance floated down from above. When Farmer noticed the snowflakes he reacted with excitement. He snapped at them with his mouth. Yet, regardless of how many he consumed, they kept falling. Then he chased the nickel-sized white flakes like a fox pouncing on lemmings until he was nearly exhausted.

While the changes of seasons were happening, Farmer was rapidly changing as well. His once stubby legs were now longer, thicker, and attached to large hairy paws. His shoulders and hips had widened and his once bronze fur was now reddish orange.

As the sun began its winter descent, snowflakes became the norm and weren't as fun to chase anymore and the earthly smells had disappeared. But now, there was a new scent in the air. It smelled like heaven to Farmer. It alerted all his senses to an ancient time when his forefathers lived on a diet of caribou meat. It was the most delicious scent on Earth.

While the person busied himself preparing caribou meat in the cabin, Farmer, Nikko, and Sally drooled while watching his every move. They sat on the wooden floor and waited patiently. Finally, their patience was met with a reward; a large bone was handed to each of them. They quickly grabbed these with saliva dripping off their lips and darted to their favorite hiding places to enjoy their gifts. Farmer's favorite place was a trench that he had burrowed under the person's cabin. While Nikko and Sally's favorite place was beside the kennel, inside a dark shed that also housed sleds and camping gear.

As time passed, Farmer continued to live a carefree life with Sally and Nikko. They played together in the snow with Ginger and others in the kennel and ran about chasing each others' brushy tails. Of course, their favorite time of day was receiving and gnawing on fresh caribou bones followed by an evening of nibbling on popcorn. This ritual was one way the person deepened his special bond with them.

One day as the cold winds swept the tundra with snow, Farmer realized many of his family members, including Ginger, were gone as well as the person who they adored. It seemed they had disappeared on a mysterious journey. Also he noticed he wasn't called inside the cozy cabin to gnaw on bones and nibble on hot delicious popcorn anymore. Just the sounds of wind called him. He felt lonely. Then a different person carrying a bucket of kibble dogfood and delicious whale oil met him. This person was quite generous and graciously fed Farmer and his siblings and the few remaining dogs in the kennel heaping bowls of food.

This was all right, he thought, even though he missed the popcorn and caribou bones, he was happy. And every day he continued to play with his siblings and a few others in the kennel.

When the sun's intense light returned and snowmelt dripped off blades of grass and onto the melting river ice, Ginger and the others also returned. They looked fresh, robust, and more muscular than ever before. There was excitement and a sense of gratification in their eyes. Farmer felt their enthusiasm and strength. He wished he had joined them on their journey. He then met his mother who wagged her tail around and around like a propeller. She was so ecstatic to see him and his siblings and they were excited to see her as well.

Again, Farmer and his siblings enjoyed a carefree life throughout the spring and summer—playing, feasting on fish and caribou bones, and antagonizing the adults in the kennel. All the while his stature grew in strength and size.

He resembled the adult males who were lying about enjoying the summer's lazy heat. Farmer grew to have a deep chest, wide and muscular shoulders, and hips supported by large thick legs and large paws. But, he wasn't finished growing yet. Farmer was a little over year old now. Inside his body, bone plates were still open and susceptible to injuries. If he engaged in any type of pulling it would injure his growth plates which would certainly cause arthritis later on.

Another winter passed as the one before. Farmer was now two years old. In late spring the person slipped a harness over Farmer's large head and chest and then attached it to the tug line. Farmer didn't know what was happening but he sensed it would be fun. The high amount of energy the other team members exhibited flowed down the gang line like electricity. Everyone howled with joy, including Farmer, Nikko, and Sally.

Suddenly he heard a command "Okay" and then they were running freely across the tundra, yet comfortably attached to the line that held them together as one unit. The feeling and energy from his teammates who were each pulling with every fiber in their being was uplifting.

Farmer wanted to mimic them and pull harder. He was ecstatic; it was the most enjoyable game in the world he thought. He loved it and pulled with passion along with his siblings, Nikko who screamed in a fevered pitch and Sally who grunted while pulling. They were lost in a world that seemingly was heaven. Never before had they ever loved such a playtime activity. They didn't ever want it to end because deep within their ancient DNA was a powerful desire to pull.

For thousands of years, Alaskan malamutes have been dragging sleds across the Arctic. Now, they were continuing their forefathers' tradition and way of life. Then suddenly they were at the kennel. Five minutes of the most enjoyable time of their lives was over. Farmer and his teammates were panting and wagging their tails ecstatically and wondered why the fun had stopped.

The person gently slipped their paws and heads out of their harnesses, petted and praised them, and let Farmer and his sibling run free. That was the last time Farmer and his siblings would feel a harness against their muscled chests for six months.

41

During which time, however, they wouldn't ever forget about their incredible run across the angel-white landscape with the others. This experience would sink into the subconscious of each dog and take root like a tree and grow. They would always remember the euphoric pulling sensation and movement. For the next six months they would reminisce the feeling of joining others in the team and becoming one being in a unified brute force to pull the sled.

During those five minutes of pulling, Farmer felt that he and his teammates were one unit that couldn't be stopped. He knew what the excitement was about and longed to pull in the team again.

As another summer and fall slipped quickly by, Farmer, Nikko, and Sally, however, had lots of fun hiking and exploring the Arctic's expanse with the person throughout summer and fall. They hiked freely with him without ever having the desire to run-off. The devotion to always remain at the person's side was ingrained.

Then one day as the cold winds blasted over the tundra, a harness was slipped over Farmer's large head, monstrous paws slipped through as well, and the harness's width adjusted to his wide hips. He was two-and-half-years old and possessed muscles from head to tail, powerful youthful energy, and a strong sense of urgency. For over two years he had played and lived a carefree life. Positive neural pathways were now deeply set into his brain. Life was always joy. Regardless of the situation, he would be a happy dog and a cheerful warrior.

Now, he knew exactly what to do. It had worked on his subconscious for six months. He was ready both physically and mentally. His bone plates were closed and longevity was secured. Mentally, he was sound and sure, knowing he wouldn't ever become sore, injured, or fatigued. Aside from learning the stop, stay, and go commands, Farmer, Nikko, and Sally were set.

As far as Farmer knew, he could pull Earth off its axis. And as long as he never learned that he couldn't, his passion to pull with deep and hidden strength would grow and prosper for his entire life. And as he continued to trust that his cheerful warrior demeanor was protected and nurtured, he would pull with every fiber and tendon in his being. But if he ever became exhausted or overworked and his strength was taken advantage of, he would certainly lose trust in the person and hold back or conserve his incredible power.

Eventually, the belief that his strength was invincible would be set as a deeply ingrained neural pathway in his brain.

I believe all of God's animals have something to teach us. The following quote of mine from my book *Malamute Man: The Brute Force of Unified Souls* (2015) can be easily applied to ourselves.

"When a dog discovers that his strength has a limit he will accept this limit as the peak of his strength. If he does not know his limit, and has never discovered it, then he will reach deep within himself and exhibit feats of strength beyond human comprehension and accomplish the impossible."

Chapter 7: Alaskan Malamutes at Two Years

Our dogs can feel when they are looked upon with love and respect. They know and understand emotions and read our body language very proficiently, thereby they rely on our body language and eye contact to communicate with us.

How might we show them we are pleased to be with them? Walk slowly, move gently, and speak and praise them softly. Pretend they are kids in a quiet classroom and we don't want to disturb their studies. They are watching our every move. We are communicating to them with our body movements and they feed off our emotions. Ideally, we should view our malamutes as equals in a team and not dominate them like an alpha figure.

A word about alpha gestures and working with dogs (or any animal) as a dominating figure. In my opinion, interacting with all dogs in this way leads to bad results. Animals treated and trained in this manner end up acting aggressively and winding up in rescue shelters. I will repeat my feelings throughout this book and in my other books because I care deeply about this subject. I firmly believe that if you want the best relationship with your dog and you want the best results from him or her, you need to develop a healthy bond that is based on love, trust, and mutual respect.

Before we go further about training, I'd like to address a common question I'm asked often: "How do you handle dogs that don't have a good work ethic?"

Commonly, but not always, a dog's aspiration hinges on our emotions. He reflects the person's demeanor who he is in contact with, whether the person is cold and disengaged or affectionate and friendly. Regardless of breed, we may find an association between human behavior and a dog's work ethic; a dog's performance often coincides with its owner's emotions. It's entirely up to us how we nurture their work ethic and influence their disposition.

To address the question more specifically, however, there are actually three answers. First, if the dog is young, it is important to allow him or her to fully mature before training. Second, once you are training your dog, it is important to never overwork them. And third, I believe in building a bond of trust with each dog. These strategies are intertwined and can't be applied independently of one another. I'll explain more by addressing the answers in reverse order.

Bonding is the foundation of training all dog breeds. Animals that lack a bonding relationship with a human will only perform for treats. Without a human-to-animal bonding relationship, an animal will not care about pleasing us and he or she will not go above and beyond what's expected of them.

I'm certain that most very young malamutes build bonds immediately with their owners. I mean, Who can resist that fat little ball of fur bouncing about on the carpet and tugging the socks off our feet? But as these dogs get older they change the way they show their affection.

For me, probably the most annoying behavior from a six-month-old pup is when he stands on his hind legs and drags his paws down my shirt causing painful long red scratch marks on my chest. This is typical behavior for a pup that is excited to see me. He adores me and is confident I adore him as well.

As the pups mature they acquire a deep respect toward us and no longer jump and shred our new down coat into a puff of floating white feathers. They will, however, still stand on their hind legs and place their big paws on our shoulders or chest and lick our lips. This simple gesture from our dogs is a very important bonding language. It shows that our dogs love and wish to please us. And that they feel secure with us. This is just one of the many simple bonding gestures we can participate in to assure our pups of our mutual respect and love for one another.

Next, I'll discuss overwork. A malamute's strength is in his heart and mind. The full force of this strength will only show itself if there is a mutual bond of trust between us and our dog. It's a trust that cannot be broken, providing it's derived from the root of goodwill and compassion. When our dog believes that he will not be taken advantage of and overworked, he will offer his strength willingly and without restraints. But if he senses otherwise, he will hold back in a self-preserving manner and only give half his strength.

Regarding the maturation of a malamute, physical and mental maturity happens when they reach the age of two to three years. Up until this time, it's important to allow them to play freely without any type of physical stress or work whatsoever. When they are young, their minds are vulnerable to being misdirected, similar to children. They can be easily harmed emotionally and mentally. So it's vital to keep their mental states stress-free and unburdened until they can handle more complicated situations.

Of course, it's good to teach our young rowdy malamutes how to sit, come, stay, play dead, and other important lessons. But, I would recommend doing this in ways that involve lots of fun for the young dogs.

Short hikes and walks are great activities, as well, just as long as it's not a strain on them physically. But pulling anything whether it's large, small, heavy, or light isn't necessary before two years of age. Not only do we risk injuring them—it's also possible to impress a negative behavior pattern on them that cannot be changed. To explain what I mean, here's a scenario that illustrates how this can happen.

Fido, the majestic malamute is handsomely built at a year and half old so I place him in my team. Why not? I figure he's built like a tank and looks and acts like he's ready to go. After a five-minute wrestling match, I finally have the harness over his broad muscled shoulders. I stand back and notice how impressive he looks with his bright red freight harness with his name embroidered on the webbing. I am feeling quite proud of Fido and I am excited to see him join the team.

After Fido and his teammates are set and ready to go, I stand on the runners, pull the snow hook out of the snow and give the command to go. The snow hook is a fierce-looking metal double-claw on a cable that holds the sled in place after it has stopped. Once the snow hook is up, Fido lunges ahead with his teammates like he knows what he's doing. His brushy silver tail is curled tightly over his back like a flag that exhibits pride, joy, and excellent health. He pulls with all his might and loves his first run in a team.

The following morning, Fido awakes with sore muscles and hurting joints. He glares at his harness lying on the sled and associates his pain and discomfort with sledding. Eventually, Fido will learn to "hold back" or pull with half his strength so he doesn't become sore or fatigued again. In a worst-case scenario he will think pulling in a team is work rather than play. If this happens he will eventually lose enthusiasm for sledding altogether as he ages.

Yet, at this early stage, when Fido runs with the team he looks like he's pulling fine. His tug line is tight and his tail is curled over his back. Actually, however, he's not exhibiting his true strength. He has already started to hold back from showing me his full potential because now he doesn't fully trust me. The sad truth is that I may never know how extraordinary he would have performed if I just had waited until he was at least two years old. And because Fido has had a negative association with sledding after his first run, he may never live up to his absolute full potential. The bottom line is that pulling in a team should be a fun activity for dogs. Underage malamutes simply play too hard for their own good and don't understand well enough how to pace themselves when facing challenges. And similarly, with a young dog, I, as the owner, don't know Fido well enough to manage his energy. I haven't provided an experience or environment for him to grow gradually into his full potential. Rather, I have blunted his ability by allowing a negative association with sledding to form.

The point to always remember is that there's a fine line between overworking dogs and working them just enough to keep them happy. What you want at all times is for your malamutes to be in a happy-all-out mode as much as possible. The only way to do that is to always avoid overworking them. Because when dogs get overworked, they instinctively resort to a survival mode and learn to hold back. Their performance will always be at a steady-paced, self-preservation, survival mode and you will never ever know what they are fully capable of and the dogs, sadly, won't know the thrill of what they are capable of.

Let's return to Fido. When he's up against an obstacle that could have been easily overcome, he will instinctively hold back his true strength. This is actually fine with Iditarod and long-distance racing dogs. In fact it's an Iditarod or Yukon Quest musher's training goal to have his or her dogs learn how to pace themselves for the long race.

But being in a steady-pace mode by default is not possible for dogs that have to haul heavy loads while breaking trail in deep snow. They need to be able to draw on their reserves of strength without flinching and with enthusiasm and happiness.

As a side note, I believe if any sled dog, either a long distance one or a freighter, is trained correctly he or she should never ever lose their passion to pull. It should remain with them their entire lives.

Once I have established a dog's good attitude toward sledding using the five-minute pulling activity when they are at least two years old, I don't ever worry about whether or not he or she is physically fit enough to pull in a team. I prefer to focus on **their** psychological health. I do that by being patient with them as they mature and let the puppy be a puppy. And I nurture their inner strengths.

As malamutes mature to two years and older they sincerely believe their strengths are invincible. Mainly, this is because their power and physical stamina hasn't ever been tested. They don't understand or comprehend that they actually have physical limits in regards to pulling in a team. At this point in their lives, the only thought of substance inside their large craniums is that life is nothing but a fun game. They love every morning when they awake and raise their muzzles and howl to the rising sun. They love pouncing on your bed to get your shocked reaction in the morning. And they always love every new and exciting day. Their lives are all about playing with you, their siblings, and future team mates; stealing your sneakers and tearing them to shreds; running; jumping; and just enjoying their puppyhoods. If this cheerfulness is protected, they will carry it with them throughout their entire lives.

Then, when a harness is slipped over their head at two to three years old and fitted to their wide chest and they join the team, their incredible strength and their belief they are invincible is fixed and deeply ingrained in their brain's neural pathways. As far as they know, they can pull Earth off its axis. At this stage, I decide that I must never allow them to realize they have limits to their strength. And I promise myself that they will experience and view pulling a sled as just another playtime activity.

Alaskan malamutes haven't survived for thousands of years from sheer luck or by accident—they have survived because they knew how to survive. Inside their minds are defense mechanisms, which allow them to prepare for life-threatening situations. These ancient mechanisms signal responses when they are being physically threatened, whether its hunger, predator attacks, overheating, or exhaustion. For example, when a malamute smells a bear, he growls in a low tone that warns others around him. Even though he has never confronted a bear, identifying a bear as a threat is part of his DNA. He will exhibit similar behavior if a wolf stalks the camp. And when he senses he is going to be overworked, he holds back his incredible strength and enters survival mode.

This defense mechanism is what I primarily focus on avoiding when running a team. But many mushers fail to recognize it, which is understandable because Alaskan malamutes have a clever way of disguising it. When they are in this defense mode, they are still pulling, yet they are not pulling to their fullest potential. It's no fault of their own. They are just trying to survive since they have been driven beyond the point that they feel physically safe and comfortable.

What if the musher isn't aware of the true strength of malamutes in the first place? Will he or she accept the defensive mode pulling scheme as normal? Some do and I have witnessed this in many teams. Eventually, it becomes the norm and mindset for an individual dog or an entire team. And then it becomes their mindsets for their entire lives. The dog or team of dogs will never exhibit their true strengths

Dogs are amazing creatures with unbelievable strength both physically and mentally. They have been known to save lives and show levels of physical power and endurance in times of struggle and hardship that are beyond human comprehension. But why are they known only to exhibit this strength in desperate situations? The desire to please in a dog's mind is more powerful than any physical or invisible force in his or her world. However, the desire to please is paralyzed when a dog is overworked and loses trust in the person who he adores.

There is a lot to learn about dogs and their hidden strengths and it can't be learned by reading one book, of course. Honestly, it can require a lifetime of devoted study and work to fully appreciate and understand these dogs or any animal. And when it comes to malamutes and any freight dog, I believe their true strengths actually haven't been fully understood by most people who work with them. One of the reasons is that for centuries the defensive or mediocre pulling scheme has been accepted as the norm. I have found that many Arctic explorers and dogsled freighters in the past never had sled dogs until they conducted their expeditions or were hired to haul freight. Even more interesting and leading to the misinformation, in my opinion, is that many past dogsled freighters' and explorers' training and traveling methods ended up being used as guidelines and are still used today. I'm not sure why this is. Could it be because the goals they achieved, like placing a flag on the North and South Poles for example, were assumed to also mean they had expertise in dog sledding?

When I have studied the history of the Arctic explorers' expeditions, I have tended to find that the expeditions forced their dogs on death marches. Awareness of the dogs' physical and mental prowess seemed to be completely absent. The dogs were used and treated as expendable tools to reach a goal and sadly not appreciated as creatures with incredible qualities.

Alaskan malamutes love breaking trail!!

49

Chapter 8: Reading Body Language

Recently I was asked: "How do you know when dogs reach their limit?" My answer is simply, by being connected, bonded, and as one with them as a team player. Stay away from falling into the alpha role; just be a team member. Read their body language and facial expressions. When you sense that they have reached their limit and you see them losing their joy . . . just stop.

What you see and hear and your gut instinct are all the tools you need to enable you to read your dog's body language. And the ability to read your dog's body language is the secret and the foundation for helping him or her perform to his fullest potential and strength.

However, when developing a bond with your dog is overshadowed by your will to accomplish a specific goal, you lose sensitivity to the dog's body language and stress points and that will cause you to drive the dog past its limit. Eventually, if your interaction is just about driving your dog to win, rather than nurturing its talents and abilities, both physically and mentally, you will undermine that precious inner strength and lose the bond altogether.

Think of it this way—your team is a musical instrument. Each dog is a string in your instrument and each string sings a different tune. Some strings are large in diameter and others are smaller. Each string requires a certain poundage or strain to be in tune. Similarly, in a team, the paces of dogs will differ. Obviously the small dogs will travel faster than the large brutes and the medium-sized dogs will have a pace in between.

Farmer and Champ singing an ancient tune.

We can easily place the small dogs in the lead and run like the wind, but that would cause the large brutes' great harm physically and mentally. Or we can place the heavy brutes in lead and allow the smaller dogs to get frustrated.

Even if we have our entire team closely matched in size there will always be a few that are slower or faster pace than others. A dog team running in sync is like a finely-tuned instrument with all the strings happily working together and producing the perfect song. So, how do we go about tuning this canine instrument?

The old saying that you can learn something in a day, but it takes a lifetime to master it applies here. With Alaskan malamutes it's much more challenging than with other breeds because they are not your typical sled dog. They were specifically designed to be freighters. They think differently, act differently, and they're built differently than other sled dog types. Nowadays we live in an age where racing dominants so training sled dogs is mostly race-oriented. But, I think it's time to slow down and rethink how we are training these guys and gals.

I mentioned earlier that the ability to read a dog's body language is the secret in helping our dogs live to their full potential and strength. Whether we're standing on the runners and viewing their tails or snowshoeing ahead checking their facial expressions once in awhile, we're processing information about the wellness of our teams.

Tails-up, happy and healthy!

51

It's like driving a vehicle in a busy downtown city. In that circumstance, we never take our eyes off the road. Similarly, it's important that we never take our eyes off our dogs. We need that constant feed of information from them.

Let's go back to the musical instrument analogy. By listening to all of the dogs' "music," or body language, we can fine tune. If the pace is too fast for a dog and he's telling us by his body language, then we slow down. We need to find a pace where all the lines are singing tight and all the dogs are smiling and have happy gates, even if while training we have to drag one or two tires behind the sled to keep a steady resistance—we do whatever it takes to keep our dogs happy.

In regards to body language, I watch their facial expressions closely. They love to pull and if they've gone too far they will show us in their faces. The facial features that I look for are drooping faces and sagging jaw lines or if their eyes aren't wide open with excitement and joy, then I know they aren't doing well. Basically, if I don't get a sense that they are "smiling," then I know they aren't happy and it's time to stop. My strong advice is to don't ever take your dogs to the point where they lose their happiness.

And what's the best way to tell if a malamute is happy? MOST Alaskan malamutes show they are happy if their tail is up. In my experience, it's a certain sign of fatigue or injury if their tails droop. Actually, when their tails droop or drop down, they're totally finished. If they get to that point, they will not ever want to pull 100% for us again.

Happy dogs!!

Sure, they will still pull, but they will hold back and won't show their true strength because they have lost their trust in us and their desire to please. This desire to please supersedes all of their other senses and is a key that opens doors to their higher thresholds of strength. We need to nurture their inherent desire to please us.

To prevent our teams from falling into a mediocre pulling scheme or from holding back, we must remember that pulling is strictly play for malamutes. We need to make it so. When we trot beside them or ski and snowshoe ahead of them, they perceive that we are involved in playing their game. No longer are we the dog driver, musher, master, or owner; we are one with them. And we share their life by playing their pulling game that they love. In life, if we do what we love; it usually doesn't feel like work. This same principle applies to our dogs. With this philosophy, a team can overcome many challenges regardless the size of team we may have.

It's important to note that every member has his or her place in the team. Some dogs are small, maybe too small at times, and some are too large for certain types snow conditions but they are part of the team that is strategically woven together to create an impenetrable, strong, cohesive unit. No dog is removed from the team for being too large, small, fast, or slow. If we are patient, each dog will find its niche. But if we treat the team members like gears of a machine, we overlook their talents. It's up to us to find and nourish strengths and assemble the team properly. And with patience, the team will grow into a phenomenal pulling machine that sings.

Chapter 9: The Two Most Important Commands

If I had a team that held back and that wasn't trained to stop and go on verbal command, I could easily find myself stranded in the middle of nowhere and facing a life-threatening situation. Let's say I'm traveling in an extremely remote region of the Arctic and sledding was easy with the snow only a foot-and-half deep. But, overnight a snowstorm dumped 30 inches of snow (this amount of overnight snow fall has actually happened to me). Now, my dogs have to break trail in forty-eight inches of snow. After I hitch them up, I head out in front of them wearing snowshoes.

But the dogs feel strong resistance against the sleds from deep snow and confuse it with a brake being applied so they stop pulling. Regardless of how much I encourage them, they are convinced and conditioned to believe that they can't pull in the deep snow because of the strong resistance. This scenario has actually happened to some dog mushers in Alaska and has led to a need for rescue operations.

The reason for the dogs being unable to break trail in this scenario is that they are trained to stop from feeling the resistance of a sled brake rather than being taught to stop on verbal command. Additionally, they are not willing to exert 100% of their strength because they have been conditioned to hold back as a result from being overworked. These two issues are a dangerous combination in the Arctic.

When I started dog mushing, I was warned numerous times by veteran dog mushers that dogs cannot break trail in snow deeper than their necks. And I was informed that the trick was to get long-legged dogs if I wanted to travel in deep snow. But, I knew it would still be impossible to travel in snow deeper than any dogs' necks regardless of the length of their legs.

This advice sounded reasonable and it was the general consensus amongst all the dog mushers I met including Iditarod champs. But being the kind of person who doesn't listen when someone points out my limitations and also being a pretty good critical thinker, I knew I had to test things out for myself before I gave up my dream.

I reasoned that if wolves could navigate deep snow, then why not malamutes? Wolves don't just lie down and die after a heavy overnight snowfall, right? Wolves, I noted, are self-driven. They want to travel in deep snow to secure game. In fact, sometimes wolves travel in the deepest snow possible hoping to find moose that are vulnerable in the deep snow. Their tenacity and drive are survival tactics. Many sled dogs have absolutely no desire to work that hard, I figured, because they have been conditioned not to.

Let's say I have a wide-shouldered, large-paw malamute in a team. We'll call him Timber. He has all the necessary tools to break trail, but let's look at how he has been trained. As the owner of Timber, I stop the team by either stomping on the brake or stabbing the snow hook into the trail. In both cases, Timber and the dogs in the team stop because they feel strong resistance and not because I also follow up with a verbal suggestion of "whoa" once in a while.

Now, when Timber feels resistance against his harness from the sled plowing through deep snow he thinks the sled brake is being applied and it's time to stop. Plus, Timber hasn't the passion to work very hard because he has been conditioned to hold back as a result from being overworked too many times.

In my opinion, an entire team of proficient trail-breakers, whether there are two or 25 dogs in the team, should be capable of stopping immediately with a verbal command on smooth ice. This doesn't mean after they're totally exhausted at the end of a long day. I'm talking about fresh out of the shoot. This is the level of training I'm talking about in order for a team to negotiate snow deeper than their necks.

If a team has this level of discipline and training and has not ever been overworked, and they have the correct physical builds, you can bet they can break trail in unlimited snow depth anywhere and at any time. That said, it requires a minimum of two years' experience for a dog or team of dogs breaking trail to learn how to accomplish this task proficiently.

Nonetheless, if they are trained correctly nothing can stop them.

Freighting and trail-breaking is all about the correct training strategy and not necessarily about any particular dog breed, providing he or she has all the correct traits to break trail.

Regarding long-legged dogs, I have found that they are almost helpless in deep snow. They can't pull their legs out from beneath the snow fast enough like a well-built, shorter-legged malamute can. So, the taller dogs stumble more often than not.

It's important which words are chosen for the stop, stay, and go commands. They should be sharp and clear. They mustn't be confusing with other commands or sounding like our dogs' names. If I could go back to when I began mushing, knowing what I know today, I wouldn't ever have used "whoa" or "okay" for my stop and go commands, respectively. But, that's what I have in place. "Whoa" actually sounds weak to me and "okay" has the letter "K" sound. So, if a dog's name has a "K" like, Kobuk, it can cause the team to go when you say his name.

I always wished I had selected a better word for the go command. I can't remember how many times I have accidently said "okay" in a conversation with a client that triggered my team to dart-off. That command has been a pain in my butt for nearly 40 years!

But, the team knows the commands and that's what they listen and wait for. I can say any other command and they look back and glare at me like I'm nuts.

Once the team has stopped, they must stay. For the stay command, I simply use the word "stay." Even though the dogs will be amped to hit their harnesses (that's called "harness bang"), it cannot be permitted. This is most important. They must sit or stand and listen until a command is given.

Let's talk about how important the clarity of the stop command must be. When we tell our dogs to stop, we are telling them to halt immediately and not when they feel resistance or when they are tired.

I've heard many mushers tell me that their dogs stop on command only after they've run 20 miles. A well-trained team should stop on a dime with a verbal command at the start of a run and without a musher applying the brake. This is important for freight haulers, especially if we want to see them pull with their full potential.

The team is on "stay" command while I search for a route.

In this scenario, let's pretend I place a rookie, Leroy, in a team that doesn't know the stop, stay, and go commands.

When I pull the snow hook, the dogs take off like a bat out of hell. They whip around a corner on the narrow trail and confront a bad-tempered moose staring at the leaders with a wild-eyed crazed look.

Immediately, I stomp on the brake, stab the hook into the snow, and the team comes to a sudden stop. The tall gangly moose steps off the trail and quickly trots into the thick forest. When I'm confident the moose is gone, I pull the snow hook and off we go.

In this scenario, I just taught Leroy to stop on resistance rather than a command. He will remember this for the rest of his life. Now he knows he has a limit to his strength and will stop pulling when he feels a strong resistance.

Now let's change the scenario and say that my dogs know the stop, stay, and go commands. Leroy is hitched in the team with veteran teammates and notices they are all sitting or standing calmly while watching me.

When I pull the snow hook they stand up and are poised to go. Yet, their eyes remain on me with their ears tuned in for my command. I set the snow hook carefully in the sled so it doesn't fall out and then I adjust the load while the dogs are patiently waiting and listening for the command to go.

Once I'm satisfied we are set to run, I step on the runners and say the command, "Okay!" All the dogs simultaneously lunge into their harnesses with an amazing force that nearly rips my hands off the handlebar. Leroy goes right along with the team, mimicking their behavior. When the team whips around the corner and confronts the moose, I yell, "Whoa!" and the team immediately stops. I then sink the snow

Farmer, Champ and Junior posing for the photo.

hook into the snow as an additional safety measure to keep the sled in place. After the moose wanders away, I pull the hook, set it on the sled, adjust a few things inside the sled, tighten my bootlace, and maybe do a few other time consuming adjustments to my load.

Whether or not these adjustments need to be made doesn't matter. The idea is to not allow the dogs to associate pulling the snow hook out of the snow as a signal to go. It must be a verbal command only. So, it's necessary to reinforce this constantly.

After the snow hook is secured and sled load adjustments are completed, I stand beside the runners. At this point it's dead silent and all eyes are glaring at me. If they could speak they would be saying, "C'mon, dad. The trail has been clear for five minutes and we're ready! Just get your lazy butt on the runners, hang onto the handlebars, and say the command!"

It's important to further reinforce the go command, however. The dogs are intensely listening and poised to lunge ahead at any syllable that resembles the command, "Okay."

Usually, I'll talk a little to the dogs close to me. I'll say things like, "Hey, Niko you're getting fat" or I'll just speak to them generally in a soft tone. This way they don't take off if I accidentally say something similar to okay when I'm with another person. This has happened too many times!

Finally, I'll hang onto the handlebars and say, "Okay!" Within a millisecond of the second syllable they lunge into their harnesses with such brute force and sheer power that it feels like whiplash.

If I'm not gripped tight onto the handlebars at this moment, I'm sitting on the snow watching a team of happy-go-lucky malamutes' tails wave goodbye.

In this scenario, the team heard and obeyed the commands. They're taught the only reason to stop, stay, and go is because of my commands and not because of resistance. As far as they know, there isn't a limit to their strengths whatsoever. Their power is pending the commands. This is important. And it is one of many secrets to tapping into their strength. When they hear the command to go, they pull without any hesitation regardless of snow depth, weight in the sleds, and so on.

Eventually this responsive behavior pattern will be a prominent neural pathway in their brains and will become their default mode. I like to envision this neural pathway like a path through a jungle. It requires lots of work to cut a path; however, once it's completed its smooth going. But it constantly needs to be groomed. Otherwise, the brush chokes the path and a different path has to be taken. So, the key is to always keep grooming this path every time we run our teams. There isn't ever a time when we can go mushing without training. It's a constant and ongoing job to keep the path through the jungle clear.

If these commands are taught correctly during a dog's first year of training he or she will get to the level of performance where they don't comprehend giving up or stopping because of resistance. All they know is when they hear the command to go, they pull. Preserving this high level of strength is where the skill and responsibility of us dog mushers come into play. We must be able to decipher what is physically possible for the dogs and what is not.

While training, I am always questioning myself about different scenarios. For example, I ask myself, Is it realistic that my team can climb this hill without failing? Or can they successfully haul a certain sled weight or travel this long?

I do this because if the team fails, it will ruin the training that has been done and it will destroy the dogs' level of performance and confidence. Or at the very least the team might have to start training from the beginning again.

With this level of dogsledding and freighting, science comes into play. There are dozens of factors to consider that affect sled runner resistance on snow. And runner resistance is a team's determining factor of what they can or cannot accomplish.

For example, sled design and material used are important considerations. There are different plastics that cause a variety of resistances when temperatures rise and fall. Other examples are snow texture, whether its wind-driven snow or freshly fallen snow. The changing structural dynamics of snow causes an array of resistances. For example, when snow is swept across the landscape by wind, especially when the temperature is lower than -20°F, it becomes as abrasive as sand. In contrast, fresh fallen snow still contains its lubricating values and has less resistance on sled runners than the wind-driven snow.

Air temperature and the amount of sunshine also directly affect runner resistance. Milder temperatures allow easier travel because there is more moisture in the snow than at frigid temperatures. Yet regardless of temperature, even when it's -40°F, on a bright sunny day, the ultraviolet light in sunlight can impart enough energy to ice so that it melts and causes less resistance on the runners.

However, the most important element that directly affects runner resistance is air humidity. Low humidity is treacherous. In fact, air humidity is the determining factor of how many hours my team runs per day. But the humidity rises and falls hourly depending on the type terrain we travel in. When we are trekking in mountain regions, humidity can differ in each valley we cross, so it's a constant challenge to keep note on humidity levels. Whereas traveling on the sea ice, humidity levels stay consistent because of the perpetual breeze.

Now, I'm sure you're wondering how I gauge air humidity levels. The answer is simply by the sound of the runners. The louder the grinding sounds from the snow, lower the humidity.

One point I'd like to highlight before we go further, I never calculate miles traveled. I only figure time or hours traveled. This is most important in freighting and Arctic travel. Dogs do not comprehend miles. They do comprehend time though. Time versus miles is most pertinent in extracting a malamute's strength. Because this subject is so important, we will fully discuss this subject in depth in the next book.

Training dogs to break trail and haul freight verses long distance racing is where the fork in the road begins for me as a dogsledder. The two training methods are starkly different and they aren't compatible.

I thought I'd share this true story with you to show the importance of having a stop and go command for your team even if you aren't planning on breaking trail. The scene takes place in the 1980s in the southern Brooks Range.

This picture exhibits their willingness to keep going regardless of snow depth-and they love it!

A Close Call at the Glacier River

When I heard sounds of breaking ice and cries for help I knew Jim was in serious trouble. I also knew the Arctic environment has no sympathy for those of us who screw up. It's crushed many souls with brutally cold temperatures and whisked away countless lives of those who have fallen through thin ice. The Arctic is ruthless. I know this because I've experienced the horrible cold-water shock that follows after breaking through ice. Thank God, I survived but it's an experience I don't want to repeat. Now, I feared that a good friend and his dogs were in the same icy cold predicament that I faced several years back.

Our adventure began on a late afternoon day in January when Jim was training his dog team for the Yukon Quest race. The temperature was -45°F when he stopped at my log cabin on Nolan Creek. Jim was heading out with his team on a four-day camping trip into the Brooks Range and invited me to join him. I jumped at the opportunity. I've been dogsledding in the Brooks Range off and on for several months and I thought it'd be fun to travel with someone. So, I loaded my gear and dogfood into the sled, hitched up my dogs, and mushed down the trail behind Jim and his team.

The trip started well with my five amped and happy malamutes behind Jim's twelve Alaskan huskies. The sun's blood red glow fell behind the towering peaks as we mushed swiftly on the narrow winding trail that led to Glacier River. With the falling sun, however, the temperature fell as well. Inhaling the extreme cold air felt invigorating in my lungs as I stepped off the runners and ran behind the sled to help my dogs keep up with Jim's fast team. The trail led us through a stunted spruce tree forest, across a narrow frozen creek, and then to a sharp turn into a thick stand of brush where a big moose was on the trail browsing on willows. After a short delay to let the bad-tempered moose wander off the trail, we then mushed up a steep hill and halted the teams on its summit to view the distant mountains. As far as you could see were jagged peaks shaped like crested ocean waves frozen still. The vast wilderness was endless. I felt I could spend my entire lifetime exploring those towering mountains and the deep valleys they shadowed.

We then pulled our snow hooks and mushed down the hill that led us to Glacier River. Jim's team ignored his commands to run across the river. Instead, they turned and ran down river. The ice over the river was smooth as glass and Jim couldn't stop the dogs with his brake. Typically, racing teams stop when they feel the brake's resistance or a snow hook stabbed into the snow. But if there isn't resistance against the dogs' tug lines they usually keep going. I figured Jim would ride it out until he could apply his brake on a snow-packed surface somewhere down river and turn his team around. Meanwhile, my team crossed and continued on the trail that paralleled the river.

As the evening dusk succumbed to darkness and the moon's glow struggled to show itself through thick ice-fog, my team trotted along at a slow and steady pace.

Suddenly the sounds of ice breaking and dogs screaming in terror shattered the night's silence.

"Whoa!" I commanded my team and told them to stay while I listened closely to gauge the direction Jim's dogs' frantic cries came from. I realized they weren't far away at all. I lashed on my snowshoes and led my dogs off-trail in thigh-deep snow toward the sounds of water splashing and shattering ice. I knew every second counted and snowshoed as fast as I could. Five minutes later, I found Jim and his huskies struggling in water up to the dogs' chins.

I commanded my team to stay, slipped off my snowshoes, and splashed through the water toward Jim and his team. His sled was wedged under a layer of ice while his dogs were frantically jumping, pulling, and screaming like they were at the Yukon Quest race start line. The cold water took my breath away and brought back terrible memories.

Nothing was said between Jim and me. We both knew we were in deep shit if we didn't get out of there quick. Jim desperately pushed and pulled on his sled while I grabbed his lead dog and tried to pull him toward shore. But the resistance from his sled wedged under the ice stopped the team's effort from pulling.

Finally after splashing around with several futile attempts to get the sled moving I came up with an idea. "Hey, Jim," I said, "I'll throw you a rope from my sled and my team will pull you guys out of this hell hole." Jim answered, "It better work! We aren't going too far on our camping trip if we have to swim all the way."

I couldn't contain my laughter. But, I had to be serious again real quick when I dashed toward shore and lost my footing on the slippery layer of ice under the water and went down. Now, I was also wet, totally soaked.

When I got to the riverbank, I found my team waiting patiently with wagging tails. I led my leader, Mitch, around so the team faced the trail that we snowshoed in on and tossed Jim the end of a long rope. Then, I yelled, "Tie this to your gang line behind your leaders. When I give the command to go, push the sled with all you got!"

I attached the rope to my sled and paused a moment to allow my dogs to regain their composure from all the excitement they felt. It became dead silent. You could hear water dripping off the huskies' chins as they stood exhausted in the frigid water.

"Okay!" I yelled. The command shattered the silence and my dogs lunged into their harnesses with a solid impact of brute force. Water sprayed off the rope as it whipped and jerked Jim's team ahead a few feet and then stopped. "Whoa!" I yelled to command my team to stop. I let my team regain their composure again and then yelled "Okay!" My dogs lunged into their harness with Jim's team going forward for another three feet. This time, at the exact moment the teams stopped on their own, I gave the command, "Whoa." I followed with a short pause and then yelled as loudly as I could. "Okay!"

I'm telling you, my dogs lunged so hard into their harnesses that Jim's sled crashed through the ice like an ocean icebreaker. When his sled drifted toward shore and Jim's leaders got their paws on firm ground the rest of his team followed.

But it wasn't over yet. Jim was starting to shiver and I figured both of us would get hyperthermia if we didn't get a fire going right away. Luckily, there were four large dead spruce trees by the shore, each of them were about a foot in diameter. I grabbed my double bit axe and felled all four trees parallel to each other, chopped them in eight-foot lengths, and piled them up.

Meanwhile, Jim rubbed snow on his dogs' fur to dry them off. When I pulled birch bark and matches from my pack to start the fire, Jim glanced at me, grabbed a jug of gasoline from his sled, walked over, and poured the gas onto the wood, spilling some on his gloves as well. When I lit the gasoline-saturated wood, up went flames in a small explosion.

The flames actually seared my eyelashes. At that point, I figured everything would be fine. I set up my canvas lean-to facing the flames and changed into dry clothing. In those days, most mushers slept in their sleds, but I preferred to camp under a lean-to, which is a canvas tarp strung across two trees that captures heat from a campfire. Jim didn't have any spare clothes so he huddled dangerously close to the five-foot-high flames. I watched him place his icy gloves carefully beside hot coals, rest against a tree stump, and sigh. As the fire's flame danced in his eyes he looked at me with icicles melting from his beard and grinned. He knew how close we had come to an icy grave. Suddenly, in a brilliant flash, one of his gloves exploded into a puff of flames that sent ashes toward the green dancing northern lights above. Our eyes met and we busted out laughing.

In 2013 I discovered several unmapped "warm springs" in the Brooks Range.

And, here's a more recent story that I hope also describes the importance of the stop and go commands.

Escaping a Crevasse

It's April 22, 2020, and I'm working my pencil across the faint lines of my notebook while a raging blizzard is pounding the sides of my canvas tent outside.

Yesterday, the temperature was around -40°F wind chill as I was skiing in front of my dog team of 20 malamutes over some rolling hills near Alaska's Arctic coastal plain. The whiteout snowy conditions and strong headwind made it a challenge to keep ahead of my dogs while skiing. Additionally, my peripheral vision was limited by the hood on my parka.

By using my GPS as a compass, I was able to keep a straight course. However, I didn't know whether I was going up or down hills except by the speed of my ski poles moving when I planted them in the snow. It was a strange sensation, like I was skiing inside a big white cloud of swirling snow.

The day before, conditions were similar, so I quit traveling early because I was concerned I would lead

63

the team into a crevasse that is common in this region.

Crevasses are created when 60+ mph winds rip across the tundra and build snow bridges partway across creeks and small canyons. I have seen crevasses range in size from 50-feet deep and 100-feet long to three-feet deep and six-feet long.

Sometimes the crevasses are also carved by the high-velocity winds into deep snowdrifts alongside deep riverbanks. These types of hidden crevasses are especially dangerous because they are usually very deep and narrow which makes them difficult to see until you're practically in one.

Obviously, the larger crevasses are lethal for a dog team and musher. It would be similar to falling off a cliff. The smaller crevasses can cause lots of damage to sleds, skis, snowshoes, and possibly even break a

Here is a typical crevasse created by fierce winds. They are like traps for Arctic travelers.
Photo courtesy of Angus Mill Photography.

few ribs of the unfortunate musher who falls into them. I can tell you this from experience.

On this particular day, traveling was fine until around noon. And then things got ugly. As the wind increased and my skiing slowed down, I heard my lead dogs' heavy breathing behind me, which meant I was too close to the team. I prefer to stay far in front of my dogs while traveling so I can choose the best route. I picked up my pace, which caused me to be less cautious. About 15 minutes, after I sped up I heard a loud crash and then my wheel dogs' growls.

Unknowingly I had skied close to a six-feet deep and 20-feet long crevasse. Both of my sleds slid into the crevasse, which stopped the team dead in their tracks. Immediately, I knew what had happened but I couldn't believe it! Even though the team had already stopped I immediately yelled, "Whoa!"

I quickly skied back to where my two freight sleds should have been and found them both on their sides, one on top of the other, in the crevasse.

Luckily none of my dogs were injured. They were all sitting with their heads turned toward me with wagging tails. I was pissed at myself for taking a gamble and traveling in a whiteout rather than stopping and making camp.

So, after shoveling steps down into the crevasse and offloading 700 lbs. of dogfood and gear from the sled, I dragged the supplies up the stairway I had shoveled and piled it up. I figured the team could pull the other sled with around 600 lbs of dogfood and gear in it, plus the weight of each sled combined (about 200 lbs.). Around 1,000 lbs. total they would have to pull out of a six-foot deep crevasse. To make their

job easier, I shoveled one end of the crevasse and created a steep ramp. The ramp also allowed the first sled to upright itself and follow the path of the wheel dogs that were sitting on the edge of the crevasse.

After my work, several hours later, the dogs were lazily sleeping. I knew I'd have to wake them up, so I walked up the line scratching heads and butts until they all stood attentive and focused. All eyes were on me. They sensed from my body language that something exciting was about to happen. I gave the command, "Okay!" and immediately followed up with "Whoa!" They all lunged ahead and then stopped. This is a technique I often use when I want everyone alert and ready. I needed every malamute to hit their harness exactly at the same time.

Then with a deep commanding tone I yelled, "OKAY!" The team executed the command perfectly. All 20 malamutes lunged into their harnesses with split second precision and pulled the two sleds up and out of the crevasse seemingly without any effort whatsoever. It was a beautiful sight to see! And it was awesome to hear those tough burley wheel dogs growling while pulling the brunt of the weight.

With this story, I'll end the first book in my series. Please continue with Book 2 where I will discuss training and managing my dogs and dog sled team. I will also discuss the physical traits of malamutes that are best suited for Arctic travel.

Made in the USA
Columbia, SC
17 June 2023